JERMYN STREET THEATRE

T0333273

15 Heroines
THE WAR/THE DESERT/THE LABYRINTH
15 MONOLOGUES ADAPTED FROM OVID

Broadcast online from
Jermyn Street Theatre, London
in partnership with Digital Theatre

9–14 November 2020

THE WAR

The Cost of Red Wine by Lettie Precious
OENONE   Ann Ogbomo

Our Own Private Love Island by Charlotte Jones
LAODAMIA   Sophia Eleni

Will You? by Sabrina Mahfouz
HERMIONE   Rebekah Murrell

Perfect Myth Allegory by Abi Zakarian
BRISEIS   Jemima Rooper

Watching the Grass Grow by Hannah Khalil
PENELOPE   Gemma Whelan

THE DESERT

The Striker by April De Angelis
DEIANARIA   Indra Ové

The Choice by Stella Duffy
DIDO   Rosalind Eleazar

A Good Story by Isley Lynn
CANACE   Eleanor Tomlinson

Girl on Fire by Chinonyerem Odimba
HYPERMESTRA   Nicholle Cherrie

I See You Now by Lorna French
SAPPHO   Martina Laird

THE LABYRINTH

String by Bryony Lavery
ARIADNE   Patsy Ferran

Pity the Monster by Timberlake Wertenbaker
PHAEDRA   Doña Croll

I'm Still Burning by Samantha Ellis
PHYLLIS   Nathalie Armin

Knew I Should Have by Natalie Haynes
HYPSIPYLE   Olivia Williams

The Gift by Juliet Gilkes Romero
MEDEA   Nadine Marshall

BackstageTrust

Digital Theatre+ provides over 3.8 million students at 2,000+ institutions around the world, with access to 1,200+ curriculum-linked resources including backstage insights, practitioner interviews, written analysis and 490+ productions.

JERMYN STREET THEATRE

Jermyn Street Theatre is a hidden gem. It combines the comfort and convenience of the West End with the intimacy of a studio. Every seat has a perfect view of the stage, and even a whisper is audible. Every seat is a premium seat.

Our tiny bar offers a selection of soft and alcoholic refreshments.

Piccadilly Circus and Leicester Square are moments away, and the restaurants, galleries and bookshops of St James's are on our doorstep. This is a secret theatre in the heart of the West End – once found, never forgotten.

In 1994, Howard Jameson and Penny Horner discovered the space, and raised the money to convert it into a beautiful theatre. Since then we have staged hundreds of plays and musicals, winning countless awards. Many productions have transferred in London or to Broadway.

This is where careers ignite, where playwrights take risks, where great actors perform just feet away from the audience. This is where magic happens.

🐦 @JSTheatre
f @jermynstreettheatre
📷 @jermynstreettheatre

Friends of Jermyn Street Theatre

Join our Friends to enjoy a range of benefits including priority booking and exclusive behind-the-scenes access.

The Director's Circle

MICHAEL AND GIANNI ALEN-BUCKLEY
PHILIP AND CHRISTINE CARNE
JOCELYN ABBEY AND TOM CARNEY
ROBERT AND LYNETTE CRAIG
FLORA FRASER
CRAWFORD AND MARY HARRIS
CHARLES GLANVILLE AND JAMES HOGAN
LESLIE MACLEOD-MILLER
DUNCAN AND ROS MCMILLAN
MARJORIE SIMONDS-GOODING
PETER SOROS AND ELECTRA TOUB
MELANIE VERE NICOLL
ROBERT WESTLAKE AND MARIT MOHN

Miranda Club

ANONYMOUS   KITTY ALDRIDGE   SYLVIA ALFORD   JA BARTON   DEREK BAUM
PHILIP BENT   GYLES BRANDRETH   CHRIS CONDON   TIM CRIBB   MARGARET CROWTHER
JEANETTE CULVER   ANNE DUNLOP   ORLANDO FIGES   GLENYS GODLOVITCH
LOUISE GREENBERG   F IRISH   YVONNE KOENIG   EDWARD LANE   JACQUELINE LEAN
HILARY LEMAIRE   JOANNE PAGE   JOHN PEARSON   CHRIS QUEREE   B ROGER REGAN
IAIN REID   BARRY SERJENT   CAROL SHEPHARD-BLANDY   JENNY SHERIDAN
JAMES SIMON   JH ZEHNER

Everybody needs their best friends, and every theatre needs them too. During 2020, we endured not only the catastrophe of an uninsured nationwide theatre shutdown, but the second blow of a major flood, which destroyed our dressing rooms, workshop and stores. Our Director's Circle and Miranda Club friends – together with dozens more in our Ariel Club and Lifeboat Friends – rescued us. It is a pleasure to get to know our supporters: we invite Director's Circle friends to watch rehearsals, attend our press nights, and hear our plans over an informal supper. Friends membership starts at just a few pounds a month. To find out more, please visit www.jermynstreettheatre.co.uk/friends/

Tom Littler, Artistic Director
tomlittler@jermynstreettheatre.co.uk

Jermyn Street Theatre was founded in 1994. A registered charity No. 1186940, with no core funding from government or the Arts Council, it has survived and thrived ever since thanks to a mixture of box-office sales and the kind support of individual patrons and trusts and foundations. In 2017, we became the West End's newest and smallest producing theatre. Around 60% of our income comes from box-office sales, and the rest in charitable support.

Artistic Director's Note

Tom Littler

'I endeavour to make him speak such English as he would himself have spoken, if he had been born in this present age.'

The English poet John Dryden turned, in his later life, from original composition to a successful career in translation. Writing in 1697, he argued that there are three kinds of translation: metaphrase – a literal, word-for-word rendering, if such a thing is possible; paraphrase – a looser translation in which the original is 'Englished' to make it feel immediate and relatable; and imitation – a new, original piece of work made with the source-text somewhere in view. Today, we still worry about such terminology – adapted? translated? inspired by? version? based on? translation?

Ovid's project, two thousand years ago, was to take these ancient stories, evolved from oral cultures across the Middle East and Mediterranean and seemingly known from childhood to every Roman, and to put the sidelined heroines centre stage with a series of imaginary letters. It's typical of Ovid – the wittiest, naughtiest, cleverest writer of his age – that he should spot the chance to express himself through these lesser-told aspects of well-known myths. Forget Theseus – let's hear from Ariadne. Never mind Ulysses' journey – what about Penelope? Ovid's letters always struck me as dramatic monologues in which one can hear these women's voices – which is where *15 Heroines* originated.

Ovid's tellings are naturally products of his own time. Our project is to dramatise the Ovidian stories in a way that is polyvocal, generous and contemporary. The classics have always been freely retold, but we are in a particularly exciting cultural moment. When I commissioned these fifteen playwrights, I asked them to take whatever approach felt most instinctive. Our playwrights could shift the stories into the present day; follow the Ovidian argument; focus on the imagery; lift off from Ovid into other treatments of the same myths; give Ovid a good kicking (he'll be fine). If a playwright was debating between a relatively faithful version and a wilder reimagining, I suggested the latter would be more fun.

There was never a request for 'house style' or a unified approach, and the writers did not collaborate with each other. Indeed, diversity – of age, ethnicity, style, voice – was central to the commissioning. (Such an aim is destined for disappointment; there are many voices unrepresented here.) The fifteen resulting plays show how differently writers can approach adaptation. Ovid is always there – sometimes disguised and transformed; sometimes in opposition, a figure with whom to be wrestled. But these are all new plays in their own right.

Wearing my director's hat, I was lucky enough to stage six pieces – two in collaboration with Cat Robey. Bryony Lavery's *Ariadne* delves into mythology and physics to give this abandoned princess glorious life. Working directly from the Latin in *Hypsipyle*, Natalie Haynes is faithful to a point but it's unmistakably her voice. I feel honoured to be trusted with Lorna French's *Sappho*, which keeps Ovid's original close to the surface but transforms its target. Isley Lynn's *Canace* is an exquisitely crafted piece that takes a dark, sad story in a fresh direction. I never expected to watch *Love Island* as preparation for this project, but Charlotte Jones' witty and moving *Laodamia* drove me to it. Hannah Khalil creates a contemporary *Penelope*, with Ovid not far away, and addresses some of the horrors of 2020 directly.

Three directors all bring, I hope, our own voices and obsessions to bear on the staging of these pieces, and fifteen wonderful actors all plant their unique footprints into the Ovidian sand. The first production of these plays was a major theatre-on-film project made under socially distanced conditions. It was enabled through the support of the City Bridge Trust, who funded the commissions, and the Backstage Trust, who funded the production. At the start of 2020, I had never heard of a 'capture partner' (it means they do the filming), but that is what Digital Theatre Plus became, and I cannot imagine a more enjoyable captivity.

I hope these plays enjoy a long life in the hands of professionals, amateurs and students. If you find yourself working on one of these pieces, indulge yourself for a moment: think what a precious thing has fallen into your hands. Stories untraceably old, reinvented and retold for millennia. You're the next link in a chain of storytellers stretching back into the past, and on into the future.

Directors' Notes

Cat Robey

15 Heroines is a project unlike any other, and in these unprecedented times it is a marvellous celebration of theatre and the people who make it. The chance to work on five of these wonderful short plays was irresistible. The fifteen playwrights each took one of Ovid's *Heroides* and remoulded them for today. The result is a stunning collection of monologue plays, contrasting in style, tone, form and attitude in response to Ovid's originals, finally giving those fifteen extraordinary women their own voice.

The five pieces I had the joy to direct or co-direct take us from the shores of Africa to deepest forest, to a teenager's bedroom, to a studio interview, to a city hotel suite. Briseis shapes her future on her wedding night, Phyllis finds her power in being alone, Dido confronts the gods, Laodamia tackles the agony of first love, and Canace defends her controversial actions. Form varies from poetry that feels suspended in time, to familiar language in recognisable settings. What unites all of these women is that they choose their fates. They take back from Ovid ownership of their lives. They are women who will no longer allow men to tell their stories; they demand to be heard. Allowed for the first time to tell their side, they hand this new canon over to us.

What strikes me most about these classical stories rewritten for today, is just how alive all of these women are; how passionately they love, how deeply they hurt, their resilience and individuality. Tragic or triumphant, these stories are a reminder of what it is to be human. Looking around our turbulent modern world, it feels more urgent than ever to search inside ourselves, take responsibility for our choices and re-evaluate what truly matters.

Rehearsals have been filled with laughter, tears and rich, vibrant conversation. Spending time with these inspirational women has been a pleasure and a privilege. I hope you enjoy hearing their stories as much as we have enjoyed telling them.

Adjoa Andoh

What if Deianaria were a footballer's wife? Or Hermione detained in an interrogation cell at the local police station?

How could Oenone pour so much love into her man only for him to dump her for a classier model?

Why are we so appalled at the thought of desire between the older woman and younger man?

Can a woman who has seen terrible sexual abuse ever trust a man again? What's the real deal with Medea, Jason, that golden fleece and the children? Stories of adventure, betrayal, seduction, abandonment, courage and survival, all demand our attention here.

How thrilling to explore the reimagined world of these iconic heroines of Greek mythology now given unique voices through the mouths and pens of some of our most exciting contemporary playwrights bringing their rich and varied perspectives to these ancient stories.

I am so drawn to these universal narratives of women's lives, refracted through the voices of women writing today, and women performing and creating today; excited to see what we understand about our lives in the joys, horrors, challenges and triumphs of these ancient women made more fabulous, more fragile, more impactful at the hands of the skilled women creators bringing them to new life. We bring ourselves to meet them in these new monologues - life and time as always, a vertical continuum; we are yesterday, today, tomorrow and eternal. I am thrilled to be a part of this exploration; this is how we navigate our lives, leaning in to the stories that resonate.

The Writers

Publius Ovidius Naso ('Ovid')   *Heroides*
Ovid (43BCE–17/18CE) is one of the best-known poets to have written in Latin. He lived in the reign of the Emperor Augustus, and was a contemporary of the older poets Virgil and Horace. He was born into an equestrian family in Italy and educated in rhetoric in Rome. At the age of 20, he gave up on a legal career and travelled to Greece and Asia Minor. His major works include *Heroides* (the Heroines), *Amores* (the Loves), *Ars Amatoria* (the Art of Love), *Remedia Amoris* (the Cure for Love), and his epic poem *Metamorphoses*, which tells of the transfigurations of classical mythology. Around 8CE he was exiled to Tomis, on the Black Sea, for what Ovid describes as 'carmen et error' – a poem and a mistake. The mystery of Ovid's banishment has intrigued scholars ever since. In exile, Ovid's major works include *Tristia* (Sorrows) and *Epistulae ex Ponto* (Letters from the Black Sea). He died in exile. The countless artists who have reinterpreted Ovid's work include Petrarch, Chaucer, Dante, Shakespeare, Botticelli, Rubens, Pushkin, Joyce, Britten and Bob Dylan.

April De Angelis   *Deianaria: The Striker*
April is an Olivier Award-nominated English dramatist of part-Sicilian descent, who has written for the National Theatre, Royal Shakespeare Company and Royal Court. Her plays include *Jumpy*, *Playhouse Creatures*, *A Laughing Matter*, *A Warwickshire Testimony*, and her two-part adaptation of *My Brilliant Friend*, which was staged at the National Theatre earlier this year.

Stella Duffy   *Dido: The Choice*
Stella is the author of seventeen novels, fourteen plays for theatres including the Bush, Soho and Lyric Hammersmith and over seventy short stories including many for BBC Radio 4. She has twice won the CWA Short Story Dagger. Her novels *The Room of Lost Things* and *State of Happiness* were long-listed for the Orange Prize. She is the co-founder and co-director of the Fun Palaces Campaign for community-led culture. Stella is a regular speaker and campaigner around LGBTQ, women's, and arts equality and inclusion issues. She was awarded the OBE for Services to the Arts in 2016.

Samantha Ellis   *Phyllis: I'm Still Burning*
Samantha writes plays, books, TV and film. Her play *How to Date a Feminist* has been produced in London, Poland, Mexico, Germany, the US and Turkey. Her other plays include *Cling to Me Like Ivy* (Birmingham Rep), *Love is Not New in This Country* (BBC Radio 3), *Operation Magic Carpet* (Polka Theatre) and *The Only Jew in England* (East 15). She worked as a script editor on *Paddington* and *Paddington 2*. Her books, *How To Be A Heroine* and *Take Courage: Anne Brontë and the Art of Life*, are both published by Chatto. The daughter of Iraqi Jewish refugees, she grew up in London where she still lives, with her husband and son.

Lorna French   *Sappho: I See You Now*
Lorna is a two-time winner of the Alfred Fagon Best New Play of the Year Award for her plays *Safe House* and *City Melodies*. Lorna was writer-in-residence at New Wolsey Theatre, Ipswich and was a co-creator of the play *These Four Walls* for Birmingham Repertory Theatre. She has also been commissioned by the Octagon Theatre, Bolton to adapt *Jane Eyre* and scenes from *To Kill A Mockingbird*.

Juliet Gilkes Romero *Medea: The Gift*
Juliet is a playwright and journalist who has reported for the BBC from Ethiopia, Haiti and the Dominican Republic. Her plays *The Whip* and *Day of the Living* were respectively performed at the Royal Shakespeare Company's Swan Theatre and The Other Place during which time she was the RSC/Birmingham University Creative Fellow. Her play *At the Gates of Gaza* won the Writer's Guild of Great Britain Best Play of 2009 and she was the recipient of the Roland Rees Bursary in 2019.

Natalie Haynes *Hypsipyle: Knew I Should Have*
Natalie is a writer and broadcaster whose third novel *A Thousand Ships*, a retelling of the Trojan War, was most recently shortlisted for the Women's Prize for Fiction 2020. Natalie is a regular contributor to Radio 4: six series of *Natalie Haynes Stands Up for the Classics* have been broadcast since 2014 and she reviews the arts for *Front Row* and *Saturday Review*. She writes for *The Guardian* and *The Times* among many other publications and has been a judge for the Booker Prize, the Orange Prize and the Independent Foreign Fiction Prize.

Charlotte Jones *Laodamia: Our Own Private Love Island*
Charlotte had a meteoric rise to success as a playwright. She won the Critics' Circle Most Promising Playwright award in 1999 for *In Flame* and *Martha, Josie and the Chinese Elvis*. Her fourth stage play *Humble Boy* premiered at the National Theatre in 2001, and was awarded the Critics' Circle Best New Play Award, the People's Choice Best New Play Award and was nominated for an Olivier award. It transferred to the West End and ran for nine months before opening at the Manhattan Theatre club in New York and being nominated for a Drama desk award. In 2015 Charlotte was made an Honorary Fellow of Balliol College, Oxford, for her services to the Arts. Her plays are published by Faber and Faber and have enjoyed productions all over the world. She also writes extensively for TV, radio and film.

Hannah Khalil *Penelope: Watching the Grass Grow*
Hannah is a Palestinian-Irish playwright and dramatist whose work for the stage includes *A Museum in Baghdad* which opened at the Royal Shakespeare Company's Swan Theatre in 2019. Her play *Scenes from 68* Years* was nominated for the James Tait Black award and has subsequently been produced by Golden Thread Theatre in San Francisco. She was writer on attachment at the Bush Theatre as part of Project 2036 from 2016–17 and was awarded The Arab British Centre's prize for Culture 2017. Her work has been broadcast on BBC Radio 4 and Channel 4.

Bryony Lavery *Ariadne: String*
Bryony is an acclaimed playwright, perhaps most well-known for her critically lauded play *Frozen*. Originally commissioned by Birmingham Repertory Theatre where it won the TMA Best Play Award and the Eileen Anderson Central Television award; it transferred to both the National Theatre and then Broadway, picking up four Tony award nominations. Her adaptation work has included *Treasure Island* and *Uncle Vanya*, and most recently Philip Pullman's *The Book of Dust – La Belle Sauvage* at the Bridge Theatre. Bryony is a Fellow of The Royal Society of Literature, an honorary Doctor of Arts at De Montford University and an Associate Artist at Birmingham Repertory Theatre.

Isley Lynn *Canace: A Good Story*
Isley is a USA/UK dual citizen playwright. Isley's breakthrough play *Skin A Cat* debuted at VAULT Festival 2016 where it was awarded Pick of the Year and

nominated for four OffWestEnd Awards, before touring the UK. Other work includes her adaptation of *War of the Worlds* (with Rhum and Clay at the New Diorama/Edinburgh Festival), and *Albatross* (Paines Plough / Royal Welsh College of Music and Drama/Gate Theatre). Isley is a graduate of the Royal Court Young Writers Programme and Invitation Group and has been supported by programmes at theatres including the National Theatre Studio, Soho Theatre and Lyric Hammersmith.

Sabrina Mahfouz   *Hermione: Will You?*

Sabrina is a playwright, poet and writer whose last play was *A History of Water in the Middle East* at the Royal Court. She is a Fellow of the Royal Society of Literature and recipient of the 2018 King's Alumni Arts & Culture Award for inspiring change in the industry. Raised in London and Cairo, she won the Sky Arts Academy Award for Poetry, a Westminster Prize for New Playwrights and a Fringe First Award for her play *Chef.* Her editing work includes *The Things I Would Tell You: British Muslim Women Write*, a 2017 Guardian Book of the Year and *Smashing It: Working Class Artists on Life, Art and Making It Happen* which was shortlisted for the People's Book Prize. Her other work includes founding *Great Wash Workshops* to help working class writers access UK arts funding.

Chinonyerem Odimba   *Hypermestra: Girl on Fire*

Chinonyerem is a playwright and screenwriter whose plays include *Unknown Rivers* and *Princess and the Hustler* which toured the UK after opening to great acclaim at Bristol Old Vic. She is a winner of the Channel 4 Playwrights' Scheme 2018 with her play *How To Walk on the Moon*, and has been commissioned by Talawa Theatre, the National Theatre's Connections Programme and Watermill Theatre, as well as starting a new role as Writer-in-Residence at RWCMD. Chinonyerem has previously been shortlisted for both the Alfred Fagon Award and the Adrienne Benham Award.

Lettie Precious   *Oenone: The Cost of Red Wine*

Lettie is a playwright, poet, author and artist from Sheffield. They won the Royal Court and Kudos Fellowship in 2019 and have just completed the BBC Writers' Room 2019/20. They have recently had pieces produced as part of the Royal Court's *My White Best Friend* online series and Theatre Royal Stratford East's audio project *8.46.* Their first full length play, *This Is Us*, had a rehearsed reading at the Bush Theatre in association with Talawa, Tamasha and Graeae, with whom it is currently being developed. They won the Best New Artist Award at Museum of the Mind in 2016, and are under commission for Audible and BBC Radio and TV.

Timberlake Wertenbaker   *Phaedra: Pity the Monster*

Timberlake is a multi award-winning and internationally known dramatist whose work has been performed at all major UK theatres, in the West End and worldwide. Among her many awards, her famous play *Our Country's Good*, first performed at the Royal Court, won the Olivier Award for Best New Play, the New York Drama Critics' Circle Award for Best New Foreign Play and six Tony nominations. She has translated and adapted many classical and European works for stage and radio. She is currently working on a new commission for the Royal Shakespeare Company.

Abi Zakarian   *Briseis: Perfect Myth Allegory*

Abi is a British-Armenian playwright based in London. Her work *Fabric* originally played at Underbelly, Edinburgh Fringe Festival 2016 where it won a Fringe First

Award and went on to Soho Theatre and a London tour. Her play *I Have a Mouth and I Will Scream* ran at the VAULT Festival in 2018, where it won the Festival's People's Choice Award. In 2018 Abi was awarded an MGCFutures bursary. Recently her play *I Am Karyan Ophidian* was produced by Shakespeare's Globe Theatre for the Sam Wanamaker Theatre and she is currently under commission there and also developing *Fabric* for television.

The Cast

Nathalie Armin   Phyllis
Theatre includes: *The Doctor* (Almeida); *Anna* (National Theatre); *Ralegh: The Treason Trial* (Shakespeare's Globe); *Machinal* (Almeida); *Limehouse* (Donmar); *Another World: Losing Our Daughters to Islamic State, The Motherf**Ker with the Hat, Dara, Behind the Beautiful Forevers* (National Theatre); *The Complaint* (Hampstead); *The Bomb/First Blast* (Tricycle); *Lidless* (High Tide/Trafalgar Studios); *Arabian Nights, Othello* (Royal Shakespeare Company/West End); *Damascus* (Traverse/ Tricycle/59E59 NYC); *Crazy Black Muthaf**kin'Self, Local* (Royal Court). Television includes: *Home; Marcella; Electric Dreams; Vera; Unforgotten; Humans; Maigret; The Lost Honour of Christopher Jeffries; Luther; Little Crackers; The Fixer; Being Human; The Omid Djalili Show; The English Harem; Spooks; Derailed; William & Mary; Holby City; The Jury; Deep Secrets*. Film includes: *The Batman; Final Score; Denial; Grow Your Own*.

Nicholle Cherrie   Hypermestra
Theatre includes: *Girl From The North Country* (Gielgud/Toronto); *Richard II* (Shakespeare's Globe); *Leave Taking* (Bush); *Mamma Mia* (Cyprus); *Jesus Christ Superstar* (Regent's Park Open Air Theatre). Television includes: *Doctors* (BBC). Nicholle graduated from ArtsEd with a BA (Hons) degree in Musical Theatre in 2017.

Doña Croll   Phaedra
Doña's distinguished career spans theatre, TV and film with leading roles across West End and regional theatres.Theatre includes: *Richard II* (Shakespeare's Globe); *Elmina's Kitchen* (National Theatre/Garrick); *Henry V, Heresy of Love* (Royal Shakespeare Company); *Serious Money* (Wyndham's); *Pride and Prejudice* (Regent's Park Open Air Theatre); *The Last Days of Judas Iscariot, Two Step* (Almeida); *All My Sons* (Talawa/Royal Exchange); *Merchant of Venice* (Royal Exchange); *Anthony and Cleopatra* (Talawa); *A Mouthful of Birds, Back Pay* (Royal Court); *Joe Turner's Come and Gone, The Riots* (Tricycle); *Twelfth Night* (Sheffield Crucible); *Measure for Measure* (Plymouth). Television includes: *The Long Song; Ice Cream Girls; West of Liberty; The Murder of Stephen Lawrence*. Film includes: *Hallelujah Anyhow; Manderlay; Eastern Promises*.

Rosalind Eleazar   Dido
Theatre includes: *Uncle Vanya* (The Harold Pinter); *Plaques & Tangles* (Royal Court); *The Starry Messenger* (Wyndham's). Television includes: *Breeders; Deep Water; Harlots; Howards End; Rellik; NW; National Treasure; Lore*. Film includes: *The Personal History of David Copperfield*. Rosalind graduated from LAMDA, winning the Spotlight Prize for Best Drama School Graduate.

Sophia Eleni   Laodamia

Theatre includes: *On Arriving* (UK tour); *TEAR's* (Rose Theatre Kingston); *The Good Landlord* (King's Head); *252AM After Man* (The Vaults); *Fennel Spiked Lamb* (The Bunker); *To Be Or Not To Be Scarlett O'Hara* (Etcetera). Television includes: *Tyrant*; *Whatever After*; *Spring in Autumn*. Film includes: *Finding Fatimah*; *I Never Knew You*; *The Good Samaritans*; *Walking Against The Rain*; *Black Mass*. Sophia is an OffWestEnd Award Winning Actress. She trained at Rose Bruford and The Estonian Academy of Music & Dramatic Art.

Patsy Ferran   Ariadne

Theatre includes: *Who's Afraid of Virginia Woolf* (Booth Theatre, New York); *Three Sisters*, *Summer and Smoke* (Almeida Theatre, Olivier and Critics' Circle Best Actress Awards); *My Mum's a Twat* (Royal Court); *Speech and Debate* (Trafalgar Studios); *As You Like It*, *Treasure Island* (National Theatre); *The Merchant of Venice* (Royal Shakespeare Company); *The Angry Brigade* (Paines Plough); *Blithe Spirit* (Gielgud). Television includes: *Jamestown*; *Will*; *Guerrilla*. Film includes: *God's Own Country*; *Tom and Jerry*; *How to Build a Girl*; *Darkest Hour*; *Tulip Fever*; *Keepsake*; *The Devil's Harmony*.

Martina Laird   Sappho

Theatre includes: *King Hedley II*, *Bad Blood Blues* (Theatre Royal, Stratford); *Shebeen* (Nottingham Playhouse/Theatre Royal, Stratford); *All's Well That Ends Well*, *Romeo and Juliet* (Shakespeare's Globe); *Coriolanus*, *The White Devil*, *Three Hours After Marriage*, *Troilus & Cressida* (Royal Shakespeare Company); *Othello*, *Shakespeare Trilogy: Julius Caesar*, *Henry IV*, *The Tempest* (Donmar); *Who Cares?*, *Breath Boom* (Royal Court); *Moon on a Rainbow Shawl* (National Theatre/UK tour); *Inheritance* (Live); *All the Little Things We Crushed* (Almeida); *Mules* (Young Vic); *The Five Wives of Maurice Pinder* (National Theatre). Television includes: *Shakespeare and Hathaway*; *The Bay*; *Eastenders*; *Jericho*; *London's Burning*; *Coronation Street*; *Doctors*; *My Family*; *Missing*; *Shameless*; *Free Agents*; *Monday Monday*; *Casualty* (Series 16–21); *Little Big Mouth*; *A Touch of Frost*; *Always & Everyone*; *Jonathan Creek*; *The Knock*. Film includes: *Summerland*; *Blitz*; *Forget Me Not*; *The Hurting*; *Dead Meat*.

Nadine Marshall   Medea

Theatre includes: *random* (Royal Court); Nut (National Theatre); *Oroonoko*, *Timon of Athens*, *Henry VIII* (Royal Shakespeare Company). Television includes: *The Shadow Line* (writ. Hugo Blick); *National Treasure* (writ. Mark Munden); *random* (writ. debbie tucker green, BAFTA-Award nomination); *The Innocents* (Netflix); *The End of the F**king World* (Channel 4); *Save Me* (Sky Atlantic); *Sitting in Limbo* (BBC). Film includes: *Second Coming* (Hillbilly Films); *Yardie* (Warp Films). Upcoming: *Small Axe* (BBC, writ. Steve McQueen). Nadine is a BAFTA-nominated actress, and her credits include some of the best drama and comedy projects on British TV.

Rebekah Murrell   Hermione

Rebekah Murrell is an actor and director. Theatre includes (as actor): *Romeo and Juliet* (Shakespeare's Globe); *Nine Night* (National Theatre/Trafalgar Studios); *Whitewash* (Soho Theatre); *Glass.Kill.Bluebeard.Imp*, *Scenes with girls* (Royal Court). Theatre includes (as director): *J'Ouvert* (Theatre503, writ. Yasmin Joseph). Film includes (as actor): *Pirates* (Hillbilly Films/BBC).

Ann Ogbomo   Oenone
Theatre includes: *The Histories* (Royal Shakespeare Company); *School Play* (Southwark Playhouse); *Henry IV* (Donmar); *Light Shining in Buckinghamshire* (National Theatre); *The Jungle Book* (West Yorkshire Playhouse). Television includes: *Krypton* (Warner TV/Syfy); *The No.1 Ladies Detective Agency, Holby City, Casualty* (BBC); *Blessed* (ITV). Film includes: *Wonder Woman* (Warner Bros.); *World War Z.*

Indra Ové   Deianaria
Theatre includes: *#WeAreArrested* (Arcola); *Richard II* (Shakespeare's Globe); *The Ugly One* (Park Theatre, dir. Roy Alexander-Weise); *Torn* (Royal Court, dir. Richard Twyman); *The Claim* (Shoreditch Town Hall, dir. Mark Maugham). Television includes: *Unforgotten* (ITV); *Dark Heart* (writ. Colin Teague); *Flack*; *Marcella* (ITV); *Requiem* (BBC/Netflix); *Glue* (Channel 4); *Holby City* (BBC); *The New Worst Witch*. Film includes: *Finding Your Feet* (dir. Richard Loncraine); *The Fifth Element*; *Resident Evil*; *Interview with the Vampire*. Indra is currently filming a new regular in *Breeders* (Sky) and recurring role in new season of *Sex Education* (Netflix).

Jemima Rooper   Briseis
Theatre includes: *[BLANK]* (Donmar Warehouse); *Orpheus Descending* (Theatr Clwyd/Menier Chocolate Factory); *Little Shop of Horrors* (Regent's Park Open Air Theatre); *The Norman Conquests* (Chichester Festival Theatre); *A Midsummer Night's Dream, A Respectable Wedding* (Young Vic); *Hand to God* (West End); *Breeders* (St. James); *Blithe Spirit* (Gielgud/US Tour); *One Man, Two Guvnors* (National Theatre/Tour/West End/Broadway); *Me and My Girl* (Sheffield Crucible); *All My Sons* (West End); *The Great Game* (Tricycle); *Her Naked Skin* (National Theatre); *Where Do We Live* (Royal Court). Television includes: *The Girlfriend Experience*; *Gold Digger*; *Trauma*; *Fearless*; *Atlantis*; *A Bouquet of Barbed Wire*; *Poirot: The Third Girl*; *Lost in Austen*; *Life Line*; *Perfect Day*; *Sinchronicity*; *Sugar Rush*; *Hex*; *As If*; *Love in a Cold Climate*; *The Railway Children*. Film includes: *What If*; *One Chance*; *The Black Dahlia*; *Kinky Boots*.

Eleanor Tomlinson   Canace
Theatre includes: *I Ought to Be In Pictures* (The Mill at Sonning). Television includes: *Poldark, War of the Worlds* (BBC); *Intergalactic* (Sky One); *The Nevers* (HBO); *Death Comes to Pemberley* (Origin Pictures); *Poirot, the Labours of Hercules* (Mammoth Screen). Film includes: *Love, Wedding, Repeat*; *Colette*; *Loving Vincent*; *Jack the Giant Slayer*; *Alice in Wonderland*; *Angus, Thongs, and Perfect Snogging*. In 2018, Eleanor was the Winner of Newport Beach Film Festival Breakthrough Artist.

Gemma Whelan   Penelope
British actress and comedian Gemma Whelan is known for her varied body of work. Theatre includes: *Upstart Crow* (Gielgud, writ. Ben Elton); *A Slight Ache* (The Harold Pinter); *One Man Two Guv'nors* (Theatre Royal Haymarket/National Theatre). Television includes: *Killing Eve* (AMC/BBC); *Gentleman Jack* (BBC/HBO); *Game of Thrones* (HBO); *The Moorside, Decline and Fall, Upstart Crow, Queers, Uncle, Morgana Robinson's The Agency, Asylum, Mapp and Lucia, Hetty Feather, Horrible Histories, The Persuasionists, Murder in Successville* (BBC); *The End of the F***ing World* (Channel 4/Netflix). Film includes: *Emma* (Working Title).

Olivia Williams   Hypsipyle
Theatre includes: *Richard III, Love's Labours Lost, Happy Now?, Mosquitoes, Tartuffe, Waste* (National Theatre); *The Broken Heart, Misha's Party, Wallenstein, The Wives*

Excuse (Royal Shakespeare Company); *In a Forest Dark and Deep*, *Scenes From A Marriage*, *A Hotel in Amsterdam* (West End). Television includes: *The Nevers*; *Counterpart*; *Manhattan*; *Miss Austen Regrets*; *The Halcyon*; *Case Sensitive*. Film includes: *The Father*; *The Ghostwriter*; *Victoria and Abdul*; *An Education*; *Hanna*; *Anna Karenina*; *Maps to the Stars*; *The Heart of Me*; *Sixth Sense*; *To Kill A King*; *Rushmore*; *The Postman*; *Last Days on Mars*. Radio includes: *Volpone*; *Old Times*.

The Production Team

Adjoa Andoh   Director (*Hermione, Oenone, Deianaria, Hypermestra, Medea, Phaedra*)
Theatre includes: conceived/co-directed/played *Richard II* – 2019 critically acclaimed first UK all women-of-colour Shakespeare (Shakespeare's Globe, co-director Lynette Linton); *Richard II*-film version by Adjoa's company *SwingingTheLens* available on YouTube; Ulysses for Greg Doran's *Troilus & Cressida* (Royal Shakespeare Company); Casca for Nick Hytner's *Julius Caesar* (Bridge); Miss Havisham for Neil Bartlett's *Great Expectations* (Bristol Old Vic). Television and film includes: *Fractured* (Netflix); *Acceptable Risk* (Amazon Prime); *Silent Witness 2020* (BBC). Known for Clint Eastwood's *Invictus* (Warner Bros.); *Dr Who*, *Casualty* (BBC); *Law & Order UK* (ITV). Upcoming: *Lady Danbury* – Shondaland/Netflix series *Bridgerton*, opening Christmas Day 2020; Director *Four Women* by Lettie Precious (Audible/45); Producer on *Claudia: The Life of Claudia Jones* – a film by award-winning director Frances-Anne Solomon (Caribbean Tales Films). Audio includes: thirty years as a BBC radio actor, writer, Carleton Hobbs Award and Norman Beaton Fellowship judge; award-winning narrator of over 150 audiobooks. Adjoa is Senior Associate Artist at The Bush; Royal Shakespeare Company Associate Artist; visiting director at RADA and Rose Bruford; Fairtrade Ambassador. Judging includes: Inaugural 2020 BAME sci-fi Award for Gollancz; Royal Society of Literature 2021 RSL Literature Matters Awards; Women's Prize for Playwriting 2020.

Gabriella Bird   Assistant Director
For Jermyn Street Theatre: *Creditors*, *Miss Julie* (also Theatre by the Lake); *Tonight at 8.30*. Theatre includes (as Assistant/Associate Director): *Rutherford & Son* (Sheffield Crucible); *Cabaret*, *Jekyll & Hyde* (English Theatre Frankfurt/Deutsches Theater Munich); *Single Spies*, *Bold Girls* (Theatre by the Lake/York Theatre Royal); *Love's Labour's Lost*, *Much Ado About Nothing* (Guildford Shakespeare Company); *The Last Temptation of Boris Johnson* (Park Theatre); *The Wizard of Oz*, *His Dark Materials*, *Wind in the Willows*, *Charlotte's Web* (Yvonne Arnaud). Theatre includes (as Director): *The 4th Country* (VAULT Festival); *Romeo and Juliet* (Guildford Shakespeare Company); *Entropy* (Park Theatre Script Accelerator); *January* (White Bear); *The Acid Test* (Cockpit); *Madwomen in the Attic*; *Twelfth Night* (The Courtyard Theatre/European tour). Gabriella is a Creative Associate at Jermyn Street Theatre.

Nicola Chang   Sound Designer (*Hermione, Oenone, Deianaria, Hypermestra, Medea, Phaedra*)
Theatre includes: *Miss Julie* (Chester Storyhouse); *Funeral Flowers* (Camden Roundhouse/Hackney Empire); *Invisible Harmony* (Southbank Centre); *Wild Goose Dreams* (Theatre Royal Bath); *Little Baby Jesus*, *The Tempest* (Orange Tree); *White Pearl*

(Royal Court); *The King of Hell's Palace* (Hampstead); *The Death of Ophelia* (Shakespeare's Globe); *Summer Rolls* (Park Theatre); *From Shore to Shore* (Royal Exchange/UK tour); *Lord of the Flies* (Greenwich); *pool (no water)* (Oxford School of Drama/Royal Court); *No Man's Land* (Square Chapel Halifax); *Dangerous Giant Animals* (Tristan Bates Theatre); *Finishing the Picture* (Finborough); *A Hundred Words for Snow* (Arcola); *10, Kompromat, Inside Voices* (VAULT Festival, 2019); *The Free9* (National Theatre). Nicola is a three-time OffWestEnd Award-nominated composer/sound designer for theatre, film and commercial media across the UK, US and Asia. As a performer, she occasionally plays for *SiX* (West End) and is a former cast member of *STOMP!* (West End/World Tour). She is also a BFI x BAFTA Crew Member.

Lisa Cochrane   Stage Manager
For Jermyn Street Theatre: *For Services Rendered*; *Miss Julie*; *Creditors*; *About Leo*; *The Play About My Dad*; *Tonight at 8.30*; *All Our Children*. Theatre includes: *Emilia* (Mountview); *Vienna '34 – Munich '38* (Theatre Royal Bath); *Snow White and the Seven Dwarfs, Jack and the Beanstalk* (Swan Theatre, High Wycombe); *Hunting of the Snark* (Vaudeville); *Aladdin* (Blackpool Grand); *Songs For Nobodies* (Ambassadors Theatre, Olivier Award nomination); *The Hunting of the Snark* (Queen Elizabeth Hall); *Honour* (Park Theatre); *Fog Everywhere* (Camden People's Theatre); *Disco Pigs* (Trafalgar Studios); *Acedian Pirates* (Theatre503); *My Mother Said I Never Should* (The Other Palace); *Land of Our Fathers* (Trafalgar Studios/UK tour/Found111).

Zoe India Dhillon   Stage Manager
Theatre includes: *Richard II* (Shakespeare's Globe, dir. Adjoa Andoh). Zoe is a 2018 Graduate of Rose Bruford College with a First in Stage Management BA(Hons). She has worked for the last two year at Premier PR in their Special Events department and has been involved on many projects from The Empire awards at the Roundhouse to the BFI's UK Film Pavilion in Cannes.

Faisa Ibrahim   Deputy Stage Manager
Theatre includes (as Assistant Stage Manager/book cover): *Toast* (UK tour, writ. Nigel Slater). Theatre includes (as Assistant Stage Manager): *Richard III* (Shakespeare's Globe). Faisa is a graduate of Rose Bruford College.

Tom Littler   Director (*Penelope, Laodamia, Sappho, Canace, Hypsipyle, Ariadne*)
Tom is Artistic Director and Executive Producer at Jermyn Street Theatre. For Jermyn Street Theatre: *The Tempest*; *All's Well That Ends Well* (also Guildford Shakespeare Company); *For Services Rendered*; *Pictures of Dorian Gray* (also Stephen Joseph Theatre and Creation); *Creditors* and *Miss Julie* (also Theatre by the Lake); the nine-play cycle *Tonight at 8.30*; *The Blinding Light*; *First Episode*; *The Living Room*; *Bloody Poetry*; *Anyone Can Whistle*; *Saturday Night* (also West End). Theatre includes: over fifty other plays and musicals by writers including William Shakespeare, Timberlake Wertenbaker, Bryony Lavery, Charles Wood, Terence Rattigan, Stephen Sondheim, and Alexandra Wood, including the world premieres of four plays by Howard Brenton, at theatres including the Gate, Theatre Royal Bath, York Theatre Royal, Theatre by the Lake, Guildford Shakespeare Company, Cambridge Arts Theatre, Oxford Playhouse, several UK tours, Vienna, Budapest, Munich and Frankfurt. Tom has worked as Associate Director of the Peter Hall Company, Associate Director of Theatre503, and was founding Artistic Director of Primavera. He trained as assistant and associate to directors including Peter Hall, Trevor Nunn, and Alan Strachan. Tom has been nominated for the OffWestEnd Best

Director Award eight times, and was runner-up last year for *All's Well That Ends Well*. Tom also teaches eighteenth-century literature at Cambridge University.

Anke Lueddecke   Camera Director
Theatre includes (as Senior Producer): *A Midsummer Night's Dream, Small Island, All My Sons, All About Eve, Present Laughter, The Lehman Trilogy* (National Theatre Live). Documentary includes (as Director): *Paolozzi Underground, The History of Women in Transport* (Transport for London); *Unbias* (Touchcast). Television includes (as Director/Producer): *Blueprints of Evil* (Discovery/ZDF); *Frederick the Great & The Enigma of Prussia* (BBC). Television includes (as Associate Producer): *The Great Euro Crash with Robert Peston, Berlin* (BBC, presented by Matt Frei). Anke is a BBC-trained director who believes that everyone should have the opportunity to experience thought-provoking plays, see inspiring art, hear stimulating music. When pandemics disrupt 'culture as usual', seeing a filmed version is not only the next best thing, but a vital and richly rewarding experience in its own right.

Jessie McKenzie   Designer (*Hermione, Oenone, Deianaria, Hypermestra, Medea, Phaedra*)
Theatre includes: *Voices of the Amazon* (Sadler's Wells); *Peter Pan* (NSPCC's Pantomime); *Chigger Foot Boys* (Oval House); *Project Riot* (Sadler's Wells); *Beauty and the Beast* (Wycombe Swan); *High School Musical* (Beck Theatre); *Anastasia* (Pushkin House). Following a life-long love of sewing, Jessie began working in theatre in 2010. Working alongside studying, Jessie graduated in 2014 from Wimbledon College of the Arts with a BA (1st Hons) in Costume Design for Theatre and Screen. Having recently left the wardrobe department at the Royal Opera House, Jessie has worked primarily as a costume maker but has also worked designing, supervising, alterations, wardrobe, and dressing.

Simisola Lucia Majekodunmi   Assistant Lighting Designer
Theatre includes: *The Healing* (Omnibus); *Lucid, Tiger Under the Skin* (New Public Company); *J'ouvert* (Theatre 503); *Driving Miss Daisy* (York Theatre Royal); *Invisible Harmony* (Southbank Centre); *Seeds* (Tiata Fahodzi). Theatre includes (as Associate): *Shoe Lady* (Royal Court). Theatre includes (as Relighter): *Mary's Babies* (King's Head); *Curmudgeon's* (Hope); *Just Another Day and Night* (The Place). Simisola graduated from RADA with a specialist degree in Lighting Design.

Max Pappenheim   Sound Designer (*Penelope, Laodamia, Briseis, Dido, Sappho, Canace, Phyllis, Hypsipyle, Ariadne*)
For Jermyn Street Theatre: *The Tempest; Beckett Triple Bill*. Theatre includes: *The Night of the Iguana* (West End); *The Children* (Royal Court/Broadway); *The Way of the World* (Donmar); *Macbeth* (Chichester Festival Theatre); *Dry Powder, Sex with Strangers, Labyrinth* (Hampstead); *Ophelia's Zimmer* (Schaubühne/Royal Court); *Crooked Dances* (Royal Shakespeare Company); *One Night in Miami* (Nottingham Playhouse); *The Ridiculous Darkness* (Gate); *Switzerland, The Glass Menagerie* (English Theatre Frankfurt); *My Cousin Rachel, The Habit of Art, Toast* (national tours). Opera includes: *Miranda* (Opéra Comique); *Scraww* (Trebah Gardens); *Carmen: Remastered* (Royal Opera House/Barbican). Radio includes: *Home Front* (BBC Radio 4). Max is an Associate Artist of The Faction and Silent Opera.

William Reynolds   Projection Designer
For Jermyn Street Theatre: *The Tempest; Pictures of Dorian Gray; Parents' Evening; Stitchers; The Blinding Light; Bloody Poetry; Saturday Night* (also West End). Theatre

includes (as Lighting Designer): *Madam Butterfly* (OperaUpClose); *Smoke & Mirrors* (Aurora Orchestra); *Sonnet Walks* (Shakespeare's Globe). Theatre includes (as Set and Lighting Designer): *In the Willows* (Exeter Northcott/UK tour); *Little Mermaid* (Theatre by the Lake/UK tour); *Jungle Book* (London Wonderground/international tour); *Blown Away* (Lyric Hammersmith/international tour); *Radiant Vermin* (Soho Theatre/Brits Off Broadway). Theatre includes (as Video and Lighting Designer): *The Process* (Bunker Theatre); *Trying It On* (Royal Shakespeare Company/Royal Court/UK tour). Theatre includes (as Video Designer): *Prima Donna* (Sadlers Wells); *The Gambler* (Royal Opera House). William is Artistic Director of Metta Theatre www.mettatheatre.co.uk and recently Artist in Residence at the V&A Museum.

Cat Robey   Director (*Laodamia, Briseis, Dido, Canace, Phyllis*)
For Jermyn Street Theatre: *In Praise of Love* (online); *The Tempest; Beckett Triple Bill; For Services Rendered* (associate director). Theatre includes (as Director): *Estimated Waiting Time* (Love Parks Wandsworth); *On Arriving* (VAULT Festival); *We The Young Strong* (Bloomsbury); *The Shy Manifesto* (Live Theatre Newcastle/UK tour); *The Good Landlord* (VAULT Festival/King's Head); *Beauty and the Beast: A Musical Parody* (King's Head/UK tour); *After Party* (Pleasance); *Enveloped in Velvet* (Arts Theatre); *Buzz: A New Musical* (Edinburgh Fringe/UK tour); *Yerma* (Fourth Monkey); *Hatch* (Park Theatre); *Freedom, Books, Flowers, and the Moon* (Waterloo East); *Ondine* (White Bear, OffWestEnd nomination for Best Director). Theatre includes (as Associate/Assistant): *Othello* (Shakespeare's Globe); *The Emperor* (Young Vic/Theatre for a New Audience NYC); *Chamaco, Inkheart, The Oresteia* (HOME). Cat is Deputy Director at Jermyn Street Theatre. She is a graduate of, teaches at and is on the interview panel for, the Birkbeck MFA in Theatre Directing. She was Resident Trainee Director at HOME 2015–16.

Emily Stuart   Designer (*Laodamia, Briseis, Sappho, Canace, Phyllis*)
For Jermyn Street Theatre: *For Services Rendered; Tonight at 8.30; About Leo; The Blinding Light; Natural Affection; The Living Room; Bloody Poetry; First Episode; Anyone Can Whistle* (OffWestEnd award for Best Costume Design). Theatre includes: *The Cutting of the Cloth* (Southwark Playhouse, OffWestEnd Award for Best Costume Design); *Martine* (Finborough, OffWestEnd nomination for Best Costume Design); *As You Like It; Romeo and Juliet; Much Ado About Nothing; Aladdin; Sleeping Beauty; The Snow Queen.* Emily is a costume designer and supervisor living and working in South London. Emily has also taught costume design at The University of the Arts Wimbledon, The Royal Welsh College of Music and Drama and The Guildford School of Acting.

Ali Taie   Assistant Sound Designer
Theatre includes: *4.48 Psychosis* (Opsis Theatre Co); *Wait 'Til the End* (The Pappy Show). Theatre includes (as Operator): *Little Shop of Horrors, Romeo & Juliet* (City and Islington). Music includes: *Clockwork Ep* – Thalash; *Live at The Unicorn* – Craterhead; *brkbts4brxt* – korghett ft. DJ Enerate. Ali is an alumnus of the National Theatre's Young Technicians and is currently studying Theatre Sound at the Royal Central School of Speech and Drama. He is a Creative Associate at Jermyn Street Theatre.

Johanna Town   Lighting Designer
For Jermyn Street Theatre: *Miss Julie; Creditors.* Theatre includes: *Two Ladies* (Bridge); *Don Quixote, A Mad World My Master, Tragedy of Thomas Hobbs* (Royal Shakespeare Company); *Rutherford & Son, Julius Caesar, Love & Information*

(Sheffield Theatres); *Botticelli in the Fire, Describe the Night, Deposit* (Hampstead); *King Lear, Frankenstein, Guys & Dolls, Queen Margret* (Royal Exchange); *Fracked!, Butterfly Lion, The Watsons, The Norman Conquests* (Chichester Festival Theatre); *My Name Is Rachel Corrie, Rose, Haunted, Steward of Christendom* (New York/Broadway); *Porgy & Bess* (Danish Opera House); *Don Giovanni & Marriage of Figaro* (Nice Opera House); *Rinaldo* (Estonia Opera). Johanna is an Associate Artist for Theatre 503, Chair of the ALD (Lighting Association) and a Fellow of Guildhall School of Music and Drama. During 2020 Johanna has enjoyed driving her restored MG Roadster, learnt how to plaster and decorate and has been creating garden lighting installations.

Louie Whitemore   Designer (*Penelope, Dido, Hypsipyle, Ariadne*)
For Jermyn Street Theatre: *Beckett Triple Bill*; *Original Death Rabbit*; *For Services Rendered*; *Tonight at 8.30* (OffWestEnd nomination for Best Set Designer); *Tomorrow At Noon*; *Creditors*; *Miss Julie* (also Theatre by the Lake). Theatre includes: *Handbagged, Single Spies, Bold Girls, Lady Killers, Little Voice, Dear Uncle* (Theatre by the Lake); *The Last Temptation of Boris Johnson* (Park Theatre/UK tour); *Three Birds* (Bush/Royal Exchange); *Good Soul* (Young Vic); *The Daughter-In-Law* (OffWestEnd Award nomination for Best Costume Designer), *The Dog, the Night and the Knife* (Arcola); *Potted Sherlock* (Vaudeville Theatre/UK tour). Other credits include: *Nora / She Persisted* (English National Ballet); *Stewart Lee: Content Provider / Snowflake / Tornado* (UK tour/BBC 2); *The Nutcracker* (Shanghai Ballet); *Egle* (Lithuania National Ballet); *Blythe Spirit* (Beijing); *Messiah* (Danish Opera/Frankfurt Opera); *Carmen* (Dorset Opera); *Banished* (Blackheath Halls); *Serse / Der Kaiser* (RCS, Glasgow.) Louie is an OldVic12 2016 finalist and JMK 2010 finalist as well as Associate Designer to Jermyn Street Theatre.

Khadifa Wong   Assistant Director
Theatre includes (as Director): *Black Women Dating White Men* (Hollywood Fringe/Fringe of Colour/The Drayton Arms). Theatre includes (as Dresser/Assistant Costume Supervisor): *Tosca, Carmen, Eugene Onegin, The Nutcracker, La Traviata, Madama Butterfly, Strapless* (Royal Opera House); *The Lion King, The Inheritance, Consent, The Girls, Guys and Dolls, We Will Rock You, Dirty Rotten Scoundrels, Mary Poppins* (West End). Film includes: *Uprooted-The Journey of Jazz Dance* (Raindance Film Festival/Rhode Island Film Festival, Dance on Camera); *The Woman Who Knocked On My Door* (LA Film Festival, Global Shorts). Born in London, Khadifa trained at London Studio Centre and Identity School of Acting. She is a Creative Associate at Jermyn Street Theatre.

15 Heroines
THE WAR/THE DESERT/THE LABYRINTH

15 MONOLOGUES ADAPTED FROM OVID

Contents

Introduction
Natalie Haynes

Ovid was a magpie of Greek myth, as we see in his epic poem, *Metamorphoses*. He collects myths and retells them, makes them new for a Roman audience, pegging them to a unifying theme: the act of transformation. But in the *Heroides*, an earlier collection, I always feel that it is Ovid who has been transformed. This most masculine of poets – Ovid literally wrote the guidebook on how to seduce women, the *Ars Amatoria* – puts on the persona of one wronged woman after another, and gives them voice.

And what voices they are. This Penelope doesn't wait patiently for her long-absent husband to return. She writes to him and tells him to hurry, reminds him what she's been through, how long she has had to endure. The Penelope of Homer's *Odyssey* is famously enigmatic: when we first meet her, even her face is veiled. But Ovid's creation is prickly, hurt, and intensely human.

His Ariadne is full of righteous anger, depicted with Ovid's trademark sly wit. She is furious that Theseus has abandoned her while she slept on the island of Naxos, terrified of what might become of her if she is attacked by a passing seal. Ovid's Dido is in silent conversation with her earlier portrayal in Virgil's *Aeneid*; his Medea interrogates her earlier incarnation in Euripides' eponymous play. Ovid doesn't demand that you know all these other plays and poems, but he does want you to notice that he does.

The women are writing letters (the collection is also called *The Epistles*) to their absent menfolk. They are trying to achieve reconciliation: Ariadne wants Theseus to sail back and pick her up, Penelope wants Ulixes to stop delaying and come home. Serial bad husband Jason is demanded back by two separate letter-writers: his first partner, Hypsipyle, and then his second, Medea.

The characterisation of each woman tells us a great deal about how her letter will be received (only in a later addition does Ovid gift us a few replies from the absent men). One can only imagine Jason slinking away at light speed to avoid the fury he manages to provoke in each of his wives. Phaedra is so filled with shame expressing illicit emotions, we have no doubt her letter will be read with scorn. Deianira sounds hopeless as she beseeches Hercules to come home: we can guess there will be no happy ending here.

The least-known women provide some of the most intriguing letters. Oenone, the wife of Paris, tries to maintain her dignity when her husband has become the most famous adulterer in history. Canace is full of regret at her incestuous affair, certain it must result in her imminent death. Phyllis doesn't know what has happened to the missing Demophoon, but she knows that his silence can't be good news for her.

Ovid's genius is to bring each relationship into the light and spin it slowly for us to see. We have only one perspective – one voice – and yet we often find we can see the causes of the crisis more clearly than the heroine who shares it with us. There are few happy endings in these poems: Penelope will get her husband back eventually, but Ovid makes us see that the twenty-year wait has been a tragedy in itself: her youth is gone, and with it, her fertility.

Only one woman seems to have an uncomplicated, fully reciprocated love, and that is Laodamia. She pines for her young husband, Protesilaos. And, as Ovid tells it, Protesilaos clearly loves her as much as she loves him. But even this couple will not be happily reunited: he is the first Greek to die at Troy, at the hands of Hector.

Perhaps the most remarkable inclusion among Ovid's heroines is Sappho, the Greek lyric poet. Although the distinction between mythological characters and historical ones is a relatively modern concern (for the ancients, myth was history which had happened longer ago), there is something quite odd about stumbling over the letter of a poet after letters from women who could call gods their fathers and summon dragons to their aid. But Sappho was so opaque that she feels like a myth: we know almost nothing certain about her at all. It is typical of Ovid that he plays around with her sexuality and its connection with her creativity: she is intensely prolific when she's in love with women, crippled by writer's block now she has fallen for a man.

Ovid's *Heroides* is one of the most extraordinary collections of poetry to survive from the ancient world. Classicists are used to having to hunt for the women in Latin poems: to infer what we can about Catullus' girlfriend Lesbia, or Horace's beloved Chloe. We pounce on details, and try to build a complex portrait from the smallest brushstrokes. And in his love poetry, Ovid is much like his contemporaries, perhaps even more so. His use of irony is so artful that it is virtually impossible to conclude anything very much about the real man from the literary version of himself he presents.

And yet, the *Heroides* tell us something undeniable: Ovid cares about writing fully rounded, multidimensional women. Although he was a man of his time (a time much more patriarchal than our own), we have this in common with him, at least.

THE WAR

OENONE: The Cost of Red Wine
Lettie Precious

LAODAMIA: Our Own Private Love Island
Charlotte Jones

HERMIONE: Will You?
Sabrina Mahfouz

BRISEIS: Perfect Myth Allegory
Abi Zakarian

PENELOPE: Watching the Grass Grow
Hannah Khalil

OENONE

The Cost of Red Wine

Lettie Precious

Character

OENONE

OENONE   Ann Ogbomo

Director   Adjoa Andoh
Designer   Jessie McKenzie
Lighting Designer   Johanna Town
Composer/Sound Designer   Nicola Chang

OENONE *to Paris*.

Are all men like this?
Are you all thieves of hearts and monsters who crush them:
savages put on this earth to
make a mockery of love?
Tell me, Paris, don't look away,
I want to see your eyes.

Beat.

(*Tenderly/pleading*.) Please...

Beat.

What is it about her that is so different from me?
So enticing?
Her bed cannot be warmer than mine, surely?
Mmh?
Her arms?
Her meals cannot dance better on your palate,
or mix well with that red wine you love so...
red wine rich with flavours and history,
or have you changed that too?

Scoffs.
Beat.

Of course you have,
you now drink white wine, don't you?
You drink her...
I hope you know her grapes and spices will not leave you drunk
with a passion as deep as ours.

I'm woman enough, aren't I?
...full-breasted,
thick-thighed and curved in the right places?
What is it about her?

What does she have that I do not?
Ah,
I know.
We know our men well,
men dark as us,
born from the same roots.
They change when they get a little success, a little status.
We know that look in your brown eyes,
the gaze over the horizon that sees greener grass.
Itchy feet
Fluttering hearts.
Cock hard for her skin tone,
Cock hard for her pale eyes,
Cock hard for a new status,
A fetish born from your enslaved minds.
Your prize,
Your, your, your trophy.
All eyes on you!
All eyes on you!
Isn't that right, Paris?
She is a measure of your success in the world.
You have finally made it to the stars.
You, you, fuckwit!

Are you just going to sit there and not say anything?
Mmh?
Are you?
I know why you love her
She erases your past.
You fool.
You hate yourself don't you Paris?
Some people from the tribe think you do,
'Nymphs belong with creatures who look like them', they say;
And they do say it, Paris,
they really do,
In their houses,
Around dinner tables,
Around campfires,
And yet here you are, Paris,

mixing with the types of Helen.
What sort of name is Helen anyway?
Is my name not good enough
Too strange on your tongue now;
an outcast to what is accepted as normal in the category of
names?
You make me sick!

Beat.

Shit, sorry, sorry,
I don't mean that.
Fuck.

Don't give me that look.
That look.
Yes,
That one...
I get it.
(*Rhetorical question.*) You see yourself reflected in me, don't
you, Paris?
You see what society tells you to see.
Perhaps that is why you left.
Is it?
Men like you leave for the horizon,
turn your backs on the nests we've built you with our bare
hands.
Our callused hands,
Tired hands...
I've seen the children she bears,
they are beautiful,
a concoction of you and her...
Perhaps when you closed your eyes while we slept,
you imagined how ours would look;
perhaps the thought gave you nightmares.
Perhaps because you don't see the beauty in you,
you assumed the world would not see the beauty in our
children.
Is that why you've left me for her?
(*Irritated.*) Will you stop for a second!

Enlighten me, you son of a bitch!
man whore!
I hate you!
I hate you!
(*Gently.*) But, but,
I love you...
For fuck's sake!

I suppose I sound bitter.
Do I?
Do I sound bitter, Paris?
You know what?
(*Childishly.*) If that, that Helen was here,
I'd wring her neck,
pull at her hair,
the very hair I imagine you stroke in tender moments,
while you *cudd–*
(*To herself.*) Why am I torturing myself?
You have turned me into this, this, person I do not recognise.
I just want to let my fists have a field day on your chest,
beat it with all my might and leave bruises I know will heal,
unlike the ones you've left in me.
No, no! (*Warning.*) DO – NOT – touch me!

Prolonged silence.

I gave you that on your last birthday,
No, take it, I have no use for it,
It'll only serve as a reminder... (*Sigh.*)
Does she know I built you piece by piece?
carefully,
delicately,
Tell her next time you enjoy a couple's dinner,
Tell her,
Tell her you are the fruits of my labour she now enjoys.
You disgust me!
You motherfucker!
You motherfucking fucker!
Do you feel pity for me?
Well don't alright.
Don't.

Prolonged silence.

We bought that together on our third anniversary,
God
we talked all night about everything and nothing.
I miss our conversations...
Do you remember them, Paris?
Our conversations?
Perhaps your high status has stolen your memories,
and buried them in roasted quail and fish eggs.
I wish I could hear you speak now...
Does your tongue curl differently because you sit around a
bigger table with the rich?
Do you pronounce your Ts and Rs now?
I bet you bathe in milk too;
too good to dip your hands in river waters because the white of
the milk makes your skin smooth.
Isn't that right, Paris?
(*Dismay.*) Oh my, you want to take that too?
Wow, you know what?
Take it,
No, no, no!
Take it...
After all, I made you that coat,
remember? Stayed up all night...
(*Scoffs.*) What, what if I, I iron my mane to look like hers,
stop eating to look slender,
hide from the sun so my skin pales,
and, and with enough lemon juice on
my green-coloured blue-black skin,
anything is possible,
I can be just as pale,
so, my kinfolk say.
Would you come back then?

Pause for thought.

I hate myself.
I hate me!
I hate (*Quietly.*) Men.
Perhaps women are better suited for me now?

I don't think I could ever go through this again.
You wept and saw my eyes filled with tears:
The elm's not smothered,
by the vine, more closely
than I,
your arms entwined with my neck
we both mixed our grief and tears together
how your tongue could scarcely bear to say,
'Farewell!'
our last dance.
I didn't imagine that,
did I?

Come,
sit with me for a minute,
sit with me on our hammock like we used to,
Just one last time,
(*Vulnerably.*) Please…
You know, Momma used to tell me,
I come from gods and goddesses,
Tribes and music way deep in Africa's lands.
She would say my forest-green skin means I belong to the earth,
to the rivers.
I, nymph,
I, Oenone,
wounded, complain of you.

Pause for thought, deep sigh.

I'm leaving,
Don't act so surprised,
My bags are already packed,
I'm leaving the chaos for the sand dunes of the Kalahari,
You know I've always wanted to go
Oh, I wish you'd come…
We'd lie under the stars as they brighten the darkness of the
night.
You'd love it, Paris… you really would,
I'd let you suckle on my naked breasts to comfort you,
to protect you like how my sisters have protected men like you

when they have shot you down like animals,
enslaved you,
when they have beaten you down,
killed your spirit.
Do you remember that,
You dumb arsehole!
God, I love you so much,
You piece of shit.
Kiss me,
This one last time,
It isn't betrayal,
I was your wife first,
(*Desperately.*) Kiss me...
(*Dismissively.*) Fine,
Don't!
I'm just...

Part of me wants to burn all your clothes,
your home
then,
after destroying everything you own,
cradle you sweetly as if you were a newborn child,
(*Pleading, whispers.*) Please come back home.

Don't tell me, you don't want to hear it,
You owe me this!
After everything I have sacrificed, you owe me closure,
I trusted you...
I healed you...
Alas for me, that love's not curable with herbs!
Should I blame my mother?
Should all women blame their mothers for what they let men do
to them?
Lessons my mother passed on to me from hers...
generation to generation...
Is her heartbreak therefore not mine?
Heartbreak from all the men who have loved and left her;
as you have left me, Paris?
If so,
then she bears the cross of both teacher and villain,

all mothers do,
and we follow faultlessly in their footsteps,
matching every footprint left behind in the sand.

Pause for thought.

I don't know what I'll do now,
or when I'll leave,
But I do know,
After you have gone,
Closed the door behind you,
I'll scribble these words on scrolls,
In notebooks,
My hands will be mine and hers,
My pen will be mine and hers,
When I say her,
I DO – NOT – mean Helen
I mean every woman who has ever lived,
I mean every woman whose heart has ever been broken,
I will write the words spoken by many women who have cried
into their hands,
felt unworthy when men like you left,
women who have given their all and wept under covers while
night became day and day became night,
Yes, those women who have received less from the men they
have loved,
I will heal. They will heal.
We will hold men like you accountable,
I will heal. We all will.

I may not think it now,
But I am worthy.
Deep down,
Somewhere,
I know I am,
I am an artist's dream.

Prolonged silence.

Is that the last of your things?
Well, goodbye then,

Goodbye then, Paris,
You beautiful bastard.

The End.

LAODAMIA

Our Own Private Love Island

*

Charlotte Jones

Character

LAODAMIA

LAODAMIA	Sophia Eleni
Directors	Tom Littler and Cat Robey
Designer	Emily Stuart
Lighting Designer	Johanna Town
Composer/Sound Designer	Max Pappenheim

LAODAMIA *is wearing an Ancient Greek-style flowing dress which could also pass for a more modern beach-kaftan-style dress – maybe there's a peek of a neon bikini underneath.*

She speaks directly to camera, a letter to her husband Protesilaus.

Hey P! It's me, your Laodamia, aka Lady P. From Thessaly to you, my boo, you're a bit of me and I'm a bit of you! I'm speaking quiet cos basically I think Mama-mou is listening at the door. Her and Baba have got me on suicide watch. I mean, for God's sake! But you don't need to worry, I told you I'd be brave and I am. I'm really trying. I mean I'm a strong, independent woman. I'm Greek, innit? But I still really miss you. I hope you don't mind me posting you AGAIN! Just to say how much I love you. I am so proud of you I could actually die. Not that I'm going to.

But also I just heard that your ship got stuck at Aulis. They say the wind's changed or something. I mean what the actual fuck? The day you set sail it was the perfect Greek-style day-blue skies, turquoise seas, church bells ringing, a load of Mama-mou's widow mates wailing, some stray dogs going mental and your big amazing ship. And then there was some drinking and dancing and singing and a bit of crying – mostly me! I know I made a bit of a fool of myself. There was so much I wanted to say to you, so much I'd planned to say, so much in my heart, but in the end, the only thing I could think to say to you was: 'Bye.' I'm so pathetic. You know words aren't my strong point. But I hope you remember my kisses too. I didn't even wear any lipstick so as you wouldn't get marks on you. That's how much I love you. And seriously, I don't think I've ever said a bye that meant that much. I hope you know what that bye really meant, all the unspoken things and love and stuff underneath it. I think you do.

And then the wind picked up and the sails billowed right up like
a big beautiful cloud and off you went. It was a wind fit for a
sailor! Oh! but it was a wind that took you away from me.
Fucking wind! And I stood on that harbour and watched you
sail off into the sunset. I watched you sail right up to the
horizon. I watched you till I couldn't see you any more. I
watched you till all the late-night bars closed and the old men
went home and the shutters all got shut. In the end it was just
me and the manky dogs left, and then my legs gave way and
before I knew it I was on the floor and I couldn't move... You
know me. I can get a bit extra... But I mean it was like I was
actually paralysed. Then your dad tipped up. And he threw a
bucket of cold water over me, which I thought was a bit
much... And then apparently I was just shouting: I want to die!
I want to die! Though I don't remember that. In my defence I
hadn't eaten and I'd drunk half a bottle of Yiayia's fig ouzo,
so... In the end they had to carry me home. Which I'm not
proud of. But it was just all too much. The saying bye and that.

And now. Look at me. I mean, look at me.

*She pauses and then takes out her smartphone and takes a quick
series of selfies. Then she scrolls through them quickly.*

Oh my God! I look like shit. I haven't straightened my hair in
days or done my brows or anything. I'm a literal disgrace.
Delete. Delete. Delete.

She deletes the selfies.

Mama-mou is on at me every day: you need to get up before
lunchtime, Laodamia, do your hair, Laodamia, put a designer
dress on, Lao! – she says I'm not a kid any more, I'm a real
Housewife of Thessaly now, I've got to up my game. And all
my mates from Phylace are like: What's wrong with you? We'd
die to look as good as you. But I'm just like: How can I think
about what I look like when my man is going to ACTUAL war?
It just seems wrong. And my mates, they don't understand. I
love them but they're like completely shallow, you know what I
mean?

Pause.

But another reason why I'm finding it all so hard – is I keep saying to myself, why are we even going to bloody war? I'm not gonna lie to you, Paris is a total fuckboy. I wouldn't trust him as far as I could – and the one I really feel sorry for is Menelaus! Mugged off BIG TIME! I mean we all knew he was punching when he met Helen but he worked at it and he won her fair and square. Then Fuckboy comes along and her head gets turned straight away! Nothing that girl does surprises me. I'm sorry I don't like her. It's not just because you went after her and she pied you off. It's not because of that. I know Helen of old, see. I once naked-wrestled with her in the palaestra and take it from me – she fights dirty. You know me, P, I'm loyal. That's what everyone says about me: Lady P? She's loyal. And I tried with that girl I really did. But I've had it with her this time. She's broken the girl code. And there ain't no coming back from that in my book. You know they say her and Clytemnestra emerged from the same egg? If that's not enough to give you the ick. Never mind Castor and Pollox, the whole family is WEIRD. Well good luck to her. It won't end well. Never trust a fuckboy from Phrygia, that's what I say.

Anyway I don't care about her. I'm just here to say: be careful, my love. And also – can we just talk about HECTOR for a minute? The things they say in Troy about this Hector: apparently the guy's an animal – they say his skills are immense. So I don't want you anywhere near him. I'm serious. If you see him coming, there will be no shame in just running away. For real. And actually while you're at it, it wouldn't be a bad thing if you just thought of all the other Trojans as a little bit Hector too. Don't trust them. They've all got a game plan. I'm telling you. Just turn the other cheek! You'll still be a hero in my eyes. Why not send Meneleus up the front – I know he's a bit crusty – but it's his wife got us all in this mess. Let him take the strain. So, in summary, baby – fight not to win, but to live. There can be nothing nobler than that. My P is a lover, not a fighter.

Pause.

Thing is, though, I've got a horrible feeling about it all. You know I'm a tiny bit psychic. And sometimes I know things before I know them, if you know what I mean. Like the day you were going, do you remember, when you said bye to your mum and dad, you made this big heroic speech and then you tripped over the front step. And we all laughed but then we stopped laughing in case you thought we were taking the piss? Well. I didn't stop laughing because of that. I stopped laughing cos I got chills. Actual chills all up my arms. I just thought: that's it, he's going to be the first off the ship. He's going to be the first man down. He's going to die!!

That's what they say, you know. The Fates. 'The first Greek man who touches Trojan soil will be slain!' And I know what you're like, P. You're so brave and impulsive, you're a natural-born leader and I love you for it. But I can just see you now pushing the others out the way so you can be the first. Please don't do it! I'm too young to wear a saggy black dress and water geranium pots for the rest of my life. No. Here's what you should do. Make sure yours is the last ship to reach Troy. Take your time! Make a detour if you can. They say Mykonos is really nice this time of year. So that way, say there's a thousand ships, yours will be the thousandth! Then stay on the boat! You don't have to be the conquering hero! Be a loser for once in your life! Just think about me, boo. Think of the two of us, getting jiggy under the sheets. Oh my God! I LOVE YOU SO MUCH!

She paces a little.

It's so not fair! You know I have like, mental-health issues, at the best of times. And this is a shit time. I can't sleep. I can't eat. I'm checking my social media every two minutes. And you know what the trolls are like. They're enjoying me being like this, oh, they are having a field day.

So here's the thing – seriously I just think – you know the fact you're stuck at Aulis now – I think it's a sign you should probably just turn back. Listen to what that wind is telling you! I know it's not my place but – come back! Please! All this fighting is nothing to do with us, and everything we've got going for us. I'm not like the other mad bitches in here – I'm not into shagging my brother or murdering my own kids or any of that mental shit. I'm just a normal girl. And I deserve to be happy. I deserve to be with the man I love. I don't think that's too much to ask.

She sits again, sadly.

I've been scrolling through all the photos and videos of us together. It's like no one else exists in the whole world except you and me. My parents are getting really worried about me. My dad said he'd have a bronze statue built of you and erect it in the back garden. But I said: Baba, what the fuck! He's not dead yet!

He really gets on my nerves sometimes.

She speaks very quietly.

Thing is I just miss you. Is it wrong of me to say I don't think I can live without you?

She lies on the bed.

I'm gonna take a nap now. And dream of you I hope. Maybe when I open my eyes you'll be back. But in the meantime, if you love me, which I know you do, take care of yourself, baby.

She whispers.

P and Lady P. Together forever.

She makes the sign of a heart with her two hands. She mouths the words.

I love you.

The End.

HERMIONE

Will You?

Sabrina Mahfouz

Character

HERMIONE

HERMIONE	Rebekah Murrell
Director	Adjoa Andoh
Designer	Jessie McKenzie
Lighting Designer	Johanna Town
Composer/Sound Designer	Nicola Chang

HERMIONE.

How can I love a man who has killed his mother?
Really? Is that what you're asking me?
Did you bring me in here to argue morality?
I have to admit I'm shocked.
The police, having the nerve to use shame
as a way to investigate murder.
You can't shame me, by the way.
If I was someone porous to shame
I'd not have made it to twenty.

You must know of my family history?
Let's start with my father – Menelaus,
a young muscleman so in love
with a woman not so in love with him.
He, King of Sparta-to-be,
the place that could be said
to be the birthplace of toxic masculinity.
She, Helen, half-goddess
because Zeus and Leda
made her, by which you know
that it was unlikely a consensual occasion.
Plenty of famous artworks depict my grandmother,
entangled with a swan,
which is not a swan but him –
Zeus, grandfather, rapist, pick whichever
and scratch what I said about Sparta,
wherever a molecule of Zeus travelled,
that was the birthplace of toxic masculinity.
Anyway, Menelaus gets Helen,
Helen gets pregnant
and I get born into royalty I never asked for.

Two days after my ninth birthday,
Aphrodite, goddess of love supposedly,

but to me an evil bitch who ruined my childhood,
promised my mum to Paris of Troy,
to settle some stupid beauty contest
between her and the other goddesses, imagine.
Off Mum went with him, entranced,
not even a kiss on the forehead for her sleeping kid,
who'd wake to the nannies gossiping
that her mum jumped on a ship
with such a good-looking guy,
much more her type,
shame she left the little one,
but good for her,
you only live once
and who wants to spend their days in Sparta?

Dad got to it, gathered all the kings of Greece,
their ships and soldiers.
This time I got a kiss on my nine-year-old forehead,
a parting gift for the coming trauma
of being orphaned for a decade,
as I waved him away I thought it would be weeks at most.

Plenty of people would say my love for Orestes
makes me a monster.
Quite likely newspapers would say
that makes *me* more of a monster than it does him,
because a woman like me should be able to guide
the men in her life away from acts of evil,
the magnet at my pure heart
a compass pointing opposite ways to matricide
terrorism suicide patricide homicide non-abiding life choices.
I should be in control of a man's conscience enough
to stop such stuff from happening
without ever being anywhere near the boss of him,
inciting violence only if it is honourable,
bringing a thousand ships full of murderous men
to a ten-year slaughter
just to win me back
just through beauty
just like my mother did, for example.

This isn't about my mother of course.
Though... If she hadn't left
then I wouldn't have been left with my granddad,
not Zeus but Tyndareus,
and he wouldn't have promised me Orestes,
my charmingly strange cousin, to marry.
We were fiancés and friends from teenage years.
He was the only man I ever met
who said 'clitoris' and meant it.
Hah, my knickers used to flood
before we'd even touched.
It was good. We would have been good, together.

Dad only knew about good
if it was pierced on the end of a spear,
animal or enemy,
bloodstained triangle tip raised in victory,
ugh it makes me sick.
In his desperation to raise that bloodstain
to the sky and cry my mother's name across a broken Troy,
he promised Achilles that his son could marry *me,*
if they won the war and returned home.
Nice.
As you know, they won the war and returned home.
Nineteen, I stand at the port.
My body gleams with the love I've had heaped upon it
by the tongues of the girls who stand next to me,
waving welcome back to cross-stitched men they'll now marry.
Princess of Sparta, I was never alone at night.

Mum's eyes don't recognise mine
amongst the other smiling girls.
She is ghostly, she is silent.
She is carried to her room that hasn't changed one bit,
the sheets the same as the day she left.
She doesn't ask for me.
Dad knows who I am. He hugs me.
He puts his head on my chest,
part of me wants to push his head down,
suffocate, suck, I don't know.

Incest and patricide has always been a problem in the aristocracy.

Neoptolemus.
Over dinner, I hear his name.
Dad tells me, get used to the way it rolls your tongue.
I tell him, mine doesn't roll for any man except Orestes.
I think he'll hit me for a minute.
I hope he does.
Spears me for the victory dinner,
roasted Hermione, melt in the mouth.
He won't.
He prepares the cars for me to go the next day.
To marry Achilles' son, Neoptolemus.

I'm not a fan of marriage at all.
Even though I always knew it was impossible
for a princess to stay unmarried if she wanted to inherit a penny,
so marrying Orestes was acceptable – a duty, but enjoyable,
because we'd discussed the way we'd live it, different.
But the whole romanticism still around it, bullshit.
Instead of congratulations, I'd always say to my mates,
when they presented the ring like a medal,
'oh god, but why?'
The why for me,
as the cars sped to Neoptolemus
and my shotgun wedding to a stranger, is easy.
Enforced. Forced. No choice.
Unless I wanted to be served on a Spartan platter
or else end up a servant in my own household.
And for all my rebellion and revolutionary leanings,
I've never even cleaned my own body,
so I have to be honest about my chances of survival.
Forced marriage in the upper classes.
Are there campaign groups for us?
I don't mean that, of course.
But I do mean this.
There is no such thing as free choice.
It's a myth as big as my mother.
Or as meritocracy. Which brings me to us.

You – the police,
and me – the aristocracy,
funded by the public and for what?
What do we do? What do we provide?
Stories and laws to live with fear by?
We are pointless, out-of-control expenses.
Think of all the holidays
the people could afford if they weren't paying for us?
I know, I know it wouldn't work like that
but it could, couldn't it?
Take the taxes spent on my family
and all my family's families to sit around
and demand marriages and kids and kingdoms
and the taxes spent on you lot doing chats like this
which will lead nowhere because nobody in my family,
including Orestes, will ever actually be arrested
and if they are they certainly won't be charged.
Let's run with this, say that yes,
without the money poured into our futile mouths
the crowds could go on luxury holidays six weeks a year,
all own a home that was warm and well
with cherished soft furnishings and fridges full,
shoes for going back to school,
shoes for fun, for sports, for comfort.
Medicines and magic would be possible
for every single person, without us.
Fucking crazy isn't it. Maybe I'm the crazy one.
And I doubt it will happen, in my lifetime anyway.

So as I have you here now,
and we are both as pointless as each other,
mirrors and smoke for a broken dream.
I'm asking you this,
to give us at least some feeling of purpose.
Doing something for others who might look to us,
for something like hope. I ask you –
Forget about Orestes. Forget about my love for him,
how that marks me out to you as a girl of hollow morality,
likely to help you find him

only to have the case files accidentally lost
and so all charges dropped.
Take this statement from me instead
and as long as I live it cannot be lost
and I'll repeat it for as long as it takes
to get the first royal in prison for rape:

I can't repel my husband from my body.

That man who dotes on his mother as the sun beats down
and rapes his wife as the moon moves clouds.
I fight him with nails and hisses and every night I regret
not training with the women of my land
so I could break his hand with my finger.
I scream all the screams of Troy
and the next day his servants bring me eggs.
I know if you don't do what I say
he will be the death of me.
Will you, for Hermione, Princess of Sparta
and lover of a mother murderer,
will you for every other woman frightened of a partner
who does no partnering, only unstitching,
fearing for the moment their blood spills a final time,
will you now arrest Neoptolemus,
my husband, the rapist?

The End.

BRISEIS

Perfect
Myth
Allegory

Abi Zakarian

Character

BRISEIS, *a woman over thirty-five. She is extremely fabulous*

Setting

A fancy hotel suite.

BRISEIS   Jemima Rooper

Director   Cat Robey
Designer   Emily Stuart
Lighting Designer   Johanna Town
Composer/Sound Designer   Max Pappenheim

A very traditional flowery wedding invitation which reads:

'Briseis & Achilles request the pleasure of your company
to celebrate their marriage.
[Day Month Year]
Dinner, drinks & dancing to follow.'

BRISEIS *sits at a dressing table looking into the mirror. She is
in a fancy hotel suite. She is wearing a massive pouffy wedding
dress. Somewhere on the floor lies the body of her very recent
husband, Achilles.*

*Music plays distantly, muffled, probably the disco in the
wedding reception.*

*Throughout the play she removes the dress, veil, any other
accoutrements, make-up, etc. She is constantly moving, doing
something to herself, but not in a nervy, uncertain or fidgety
way – every action she makes is deliberate, thought through, by
design.*

My mother, god rest her murdered soul – but that's another
story somewhere begging to be told – gave me an unnecessarily
convoluted name. Briseis. I know, right? No one can ever
pronounce it when they see it writ. So of course it got
abbreviated. I went through childhood being called a cheese.
Which is quite fashionable now, so I understand. The name, not
the cheese. Me and my fourteen sisters all saddled with names
not particularly well-known... perhaps a few. We'd take bets on
which of us had the most unrecognisable name; imagined
futures for ourselves, wrote epic stories, made libraries in our
heads: the safest space for us all back then.

Pause.

One by one they left.

Longer pause.

When I was little I used to fear the Arrival of the Aunts. Their
visits would herald dress-up and my mother would strive to
dollify me beyond recognition. My recognition of myself, that
is. I never looked how she wanted until the few times she could
get her hands on me and add lace, somehow. In my hair, on the
edge of a dress, those awful pointless ankle socks with the ruff.
Pointless lace trim on everything. But I would stand, let her
gussy me. She usually offered me things to get me to comply;
some coins. Once, when it was a very big deal – I do remember
there being fireworks, distantly – she gave me a whole ten
pounds. Being small and concerned with currency I let her put
me in a monstrosity that equalled this thing I'm wearing now. I
took the money up front; made sure to place it carefully in my
small tin box, locked it. Mother flouncing my hair even as I did
other things; so concerned was she with me looking like a tiny
confection she didn't notice me drawing birds in my book, or
picking at the scab on my knee, or eating a linty sweet I'd found
stuck to the bottom of the horrendous shoes she made me wear.

Pause.

I was still sucking that sweet as I entered the front room, now
full of people, relatives, whatever event this was, was important
enough to warrant the full family gathering. The uncles, half-
brothers, cousins with barely fluff on their faces... all those
eyes, all that maleness directed at me, suddenly. Looking at me
in a way that caused me to prickle with heat under all the frou.
Why is it I somehow knew? Even then – at what? eleven?
twelve? Even then I knew what it was to be prepared.

Pause.

But a child. After all. I would tear my hair out in clumps; leave
piles silently for my mother. So she would know I objected.

Pause.

To be pretty was the greatest prize. Above all else. To be
wanted, but not for my skill at drawing the birds I would watch
from my window; their wings blurred on my page – I would rub
hard on the thick pencil lines so the wings beat faster, then,
fingers filthy with graphite, I would solemnly drag the tips

across my face. Creating camouflage, dirt, full filthy pores. To be pretty was an art, taught. I did not apply myself.

A heavy pause here, and then:

Smile!
You look so much prettier when you do!
Smile!
It might never happen!
Smile!
Frowning gives you more lines on your face!
Smile!
Do you have to look so angry?
Smile!
Smile!
Smile!

Her face is a rictus smile, her eyes are blank. She stays like this for a few seconds then blinks.

Turns out the party was for me, after all.

Pause, she is repulsed at the memory.

I was gone within the hour. Made a tiny wife. I remember the sting, the bolt I did not want. My mother would talk of honour. Ha. Honour is such a vile word. Such a vile thing. Why is it men are born with it? But we women are granted it for behaving. Honour? I received no such thing.

She starts the long and complicated process of removing the wedding dress; she does this like a forensics expert might.

He was so very old. To me, at least. He called me his princess, as if that would make the wet legs, the invasion, any less disgusting. So many stairs in that big house; my calves defined daily. Sometimes I would let him catch me – not for any reason other than to fool his heart of course; and what a heart it was.

She is wistful.

Enlarged. Diseased.

Tiny pause.

Myocardially infarcted.

She thinks.

When we buried him I felt all those eyes on me again.

Pause.

But I took the opportunity to return to my studies; thankful for the small financial cushion. Plus the house. I got a lot of visitors; people pay their respects in so many different ways.

The dress is off now. She regards it.

I remember a conversation with a tutor – she may have been a visiting academic, they usually were – she told me that the use of the wedding dress was a trope, and a tired one at that. Stung, and not being from one of those families where you inherit confidence as a birthright, I immediately flung myself into the metaphysical; imagining my earlier gaucheness to be a hideous footnote to the self. But I tell you what, this dress is real. It serves a purpose. If only to soak up the mess he's made on the floor.

Pause.

(*Singing, or humming.*) As long as he needs me –

Quick beat.

– we met at university. I say 'met'… I was halfway through an engineering degree but already taking an interest in finance and up he pops: six pack, bi-curious. We had fun. Everything is so deliciously fluid when you're left to manage your own timetables. Then there was Pat… he was always so jealous of me; god it was tedious – he never believed me when I said I was happy to share. They did make a gorgeous couple though; those rippling torsos, glorious nipples for days…

She savours the memory.

A real shame that hit and run did such a number on his fine body.

She gestures to somewhere in the room, floor-wise.

This one was a mess; bereft. I did what I could but I'd just been offered a position overseas and I wanted to impress my new boss. She was very demanding and it was fun, for a while. Years pass so quickly when you're a woman; time never lets you forget yourself, and before you know it you're ten years older and you know all there is to know about the stud-farm business.

Mainly that there is nothing between a man's legs that you will not find between your own. Holding power there, holding it tight.

Pause.

And then when he got back in touch I was delighted. Not that I didn't know what he'd been up to in the intervening years; the war, the rapid rise in rank, the other women, other men. So when I read that he was a keen horseman it was only a matter of time before I made sure to cross his path again. We… oh what's that phrase?

Clicks her fingers, casting about for the word, finds it.

Reconnected! Yes. That's it. We reconnected. The boss wasn't too happy about me leaving, but by then the takeover was nearly complete. She took it well, all things considered, and I made sure she had enough to live out her days in ease. I owed her that, at least. Which is why it was such a shame she didn't live to see the wedding. She'd have loved it; all this fuss, lace. Like my mother in that respect. Seeing me gussied up. Neither of them realising how little it means.

She is pulling on the suit trousers here, then picks up her phone, checks something on it, checks the time.

God, we women run through these thin tales like a sparse thread don't we? My fourteen sisters off being foils, being stoic, being dead. Being anything but the fabric the needle goes through, made into something.

I would love to visit them. If any of them are still alive. Who knows? I travel constantly, searching for them, turning the pages of every book, every journal, clicking through articles. With every scroll my eyes wait for their names – will my sisters ever come? I miss them. The platinum thread should leap. We should be complete.

She finally removes the wig, she has short hair underneath. She observes the wig in her hands, holds it up on the fist of her hand.

To shed a skin once is hard enough. To do it continually, slaking yourself, removing what you were, could be, could never be... that takes immense courage and skill. Time is stretched over our bodies; so much time. But time is foolish. It never thought the gristle, the gut, the rent, red stuff could ever command such power. Sugar, on an open wound, stings just as much as salt.

Beat.

Here we go again.

Pause.

Perhaps I will stay a little longer next time, wherever it is I end. Perhaps I will see who notices me; and judge them by what they intend.

She looks down, observes Achilles' body. She drops/places the wig on his body with a deliberate motion.

He signed everything I put in front of him. They all do. I got everything, even those damn horses. To be honest with you I'm amazed at how easy it is. The slot, the currency exchange. As of now my folio stands at sixteen-point-five million. And that's without the assets. So I feel very secure. Perhaps I'll start a foundation. I like the idea of my name on things. My name in copperplate... or a new font; the font could carry my name; describe the thing it is by being the thing it is. Oh how exhilarating that is! Imagine. A new language. One dedicated to me.

She makes a call to reception.

Hi, yes... Room 237. Could you order a car for me – for the airport please. Five minutes. Lovely. Thank you so much.

She puts the phone down.

It has always been said: this is a man's world.

Pause.

I disagree.

She gathers her coat, bag, passport, etc.

Maybe I'll go to Paris next.

She thinks.

Maybe.

BRISEIS *is now clean-faced, short-haired, dressed in a loose, stylish trouser suit. She is both striking and yet unseen; a happy blank canvas.*

In the doorway, almost gone, broad smile of freedom on her face.

This is the one where I leave, again. Alive, intact. With money, a security I made for myself. The one where I leave a trace that is not greying on a slab, or slick with my own blood. Or even just disappeared halfway through; not even a footnote in a story full of swollen dicks. Yes. In the greatest oral tradition I tell you my story, up to this moment. But it will continue, I promise.

This is the one I put down in words, in rude health, entirely sane. This is the one where I stoke the canon, light a fuse. Where my aim is... well, the joy is in not knowing. Rather, the joy is being free to wander into a history I alone will make.

She stares at us, absolutely certain. Then leaves, shutting the door behind her.

The End.

PENELOPE

Watching the Grass Grow

Hannah Khalil

Character

PENELOPE (PEN)

PENELOPE   Gemma Whelan

Director   Tom Littler
Designer   Louie Whitemore
Lighting Designer   Johanna Town
Composer/Sound Designer   Max Pappenheim

PEN *is writing a text. There's an electric plug on the table in front of her.*

Five texts. And three voicemails I've sent. So far. Today. God knows how many since Friday. And nothing. But that's okay. Because I don't want a response. I just want you home. So get the fuck home.
Now.
Where are you? Where are you? Where the fuck are you? You tardy bastard.

A beat.

Too much?

A beat.

Too much.

A beat.

Delete.

She deletes the message and puts down the phone.

Patience, Pen. Patience. He'll be back today. He has to be.

A beat.

Jesus. I wish… I wish… that prick of a boss of yours had been drowned – drowned on that fucking schooner.
That'd serve him right for organising a work jolly in the middle of a pandemic.
I wish the fucking sail had hit him in the head and knocked him in the angry water and he had sunk like a cold stone. Then you'd have come home. And been in bed with me. Not over there. And I'd have slept this week, not lain awake at night counting the days, watching the grass grow and wondering and worrying and –

A beat.

Because that's where worry lives. In the dark. In the night. And
love is the worst thing in the world because it makes you
scared. It gives you fears – anxious fears. Consumes.
Transforms.

She glances at the phone.

The things I imagined.
Imagine.
Ridiculous.
Because you're not a child – you're not a boy. And yet.
You've never been a strong swimmer…
And people fall when they climb rocks – it happens.
And clay-pigeon shoots have real guns don't they?
Archery arrows can go astray.
And I don't trust one of them. Not one of them to look out for
you. Not Big Ant, not Pub, or Heel. They're all a waste of space.
Neanderthals. Barely two brain cells to rub together. Warriors
you call them. Thugs is what they are. Self-serving thugs.

A beat.
She calms herself.

Calm, Pen, calm – he got through task one. The sailing – thank
God. Survived unscathed. Better than survived, was victorious.
The wives' WhatsApp was on fire. Relieved. I mean imagine
having to hear it from others… how could that prick forbid you
using your phones? Actually taking them off you when you
arrived. Bastard. I would have thought you were lying if the
others hadn't said the same – and so we set up the WhatsApp –
women are resourceful. And we all feed in the news. The dribs
and drabs we get. Not that I've had any. From you.

A beat.

Heel's Brie had news though. He'd found a payphone by all
accounts. How he knew Brie's number off by heart I don't
know. That's real love. Would you know mine I wonder?…
Anyway she said you had a nightmare with the tents. That
you'd all come back from your sailing – a bit drunk and tired
but alive thank Christ – and that bastard boss of yours told you
to put up the tents but didn't leave any instructions.

So you all set to work.

And arguing.

And failing, this pathetic test he'd set. I mean what putting up a fucking tent has to do with advertising I don't know, but Brie says it all gets rather heated and Heel tries to take over, and he's got the mallet and he's telling everyone what's what – and another guy from a nearby tent – local she said, from over there – who's been watching and laughing comes over to offer some advice and gets chased off with the same mallet. Then of course it starts to rain and Pub wants to get to the pub and the bloody tent's not up yet. But Brie said that it was you who figured it all out, who got those guy ropes secure and pegs in and saved the day.

Proper heroic.

I was proud.

But angry I was hearing it second hand.

A beat.
She checks her phone.

And then Mac tells me you've emailed him.

Pictures.

Now don't get me wrong, I'm delighted you have managed to get a message to your son – borrowed someone else's phone maybe? Or an internet café, do they still exist? But again I wonder why not me? Oh I know why. Knew I wouldn't be as impressed as him. And that I'd reply. Want more. I had to threaten Mac to get the whole story. But get it I did.

Picture one: You all green on a boat

Reckons your team won the sailing. Great.

Picture two: You all proud in front of the tent

You succeeded. This I already know.

Picture three: You all drinking foreign beer

Again I'd guessed – the pub – and then

Picture four: You with a packet of brioche and a bloody face. This panicked me. Mac tried to reassure me… told me when you're back at the site after a skinful the boss sets more challenges. And these fucking ridiculous drunken challenges involve running amok in the dark, pilfering things from other tents. Puerile. You all have to bring back a trophy. And you and

Big Ant volunteer, go lumbering about – nearly raze the whole
camp in your ridiculous mission. Come back with the spoils – a
packet of brioche and a camp stool. And then you get a thick lip
for your trouble from the owner of the stool. Who you woke up.
You arse.

You're pissing about in a field like a teenager while I'm here
waiting for you. And worrying.

And washing. Our sheets – the wedding ones, Egyptian cotton,
your favourite. I washed them thinking you'd be home Friday –
as you promised. But you didn't come so I washed them again
yesterday – same story and so, on the machine went again today
and I'll keep washing them until you get home. Because I know
how you love those sheets. And coming home to a clean bed,
well that's what it's all about isn't it? If you won't come home
for your wife, come home for the sheets…

A beat.
She checks the phone.

I'm getting old waiting.

Turning into a nag.

This is not me.

We were always independent before – separate nights out – with
our own mates – but you'd end up chasing me round town using
'Find a Friend' on your phone. Me blocking you, but then turning
up at The Boar's Head at the end of the night knowing you'd be
there… And you were always surprised. The way your face lit up
when you saw me. Joy. Like you really, really loved me. And the
kisses. I knew where you'd be. Knew we'd be together in the end
– and so did you… even if we started the night separately…
But through all this – being home with you all the time… *us*. I've
gotten used to it. The constant togetherness. Sappy I know. But I
miss you. Even started mentioning you on work calls – 'he'll be
home Friday' – pathetic – though not as pathetic as *their* lies about
their waist measurements, I'm telling you being a virtual
dressmaker is IMPOSSIBLE – no one's honest about their
lockdown lard-arses, but if the dress doesn't fit I get it in the neck.
Trying to guesstimate saddle baggage on Zoom is an art in itself.

A beat.

You see that's me – not this – this worrying, anxious…
It's true.
And when I don't hear from you I start texting and calling
everyone. Family, friends, I even tried your Granny Margaret –
you've been known to give her a drunken call in the past. You
know *her* number. And I get snippets. But that's not enough. To
stop my worries. My wonderings. I fear everything insanely.
Yes.
The swimming, the climbing, the guns, the arrows – though I
know all that is done with now. That you survived. That. Six
days you said, six. Works outing. Team building. Network.
Make connections. But connections with who?
I fear that insanely too.
Foreign love.
Flame-haired beauties.
Ridiculous. Insane. And yet. Why not?
It's not only men over there is it? Where you are. And we're not
unattractive – you and I. Not young but not unattractive
either… And people notice. Don't they?

A beat.

Like Mel next door. He keeps asking where you are – I told him
away – work – back soon. But he's counting the days too.
Keeps 'checking in'… from a distance of course. And Geoff
opposite keeps twitching his curtains every time I put out the
rubbish. I'm watched. And I'm getting sick of it.

A beat.

You know I woke up yesterday to the sound of a lawnmower
outside the window and it was him. Mel.
Mowing our lawn.
Your lawn.
I was so shocked I leaned out of the window in my nightie.
Half-asleep. Didn't know what was going on. He got an eyeful.
Rather pleased about it I think. I ran to get my dressing gown.
Went outside in my slippers. 'What are you doing?'
That's my lawn.
His lawn.
His job.

'I was doing my own,' he says. 'And thought yours needed a bit of attention – no trouble,' he says.

No trouble.

And he eyes my dressing-gown cord. From a distance. And says, 'He is coming back isn't he?' And I say 'YES YES HE IS COMING BACK.' 'But it's been more than a week now hasn't it?' he says, and I want to punch him in the face because I don't want him on my lawn – our lawn counting, counting days that you have been absent – away from me.

And guessing that you have failed to contact me – even once – in all that time. Your phone a casualty of – what? The water? The climbing? A missing charger?

Messages I get

From others

The wives' WhatsApp

Even the bastard boss.

Apologising for the delay – cancelled flights.

But nothing from you.

While I worry –

and imagine

things…

you –

coughing

And sweating

In a hotel room.

Near the airport.

Alone.

And I no longer fear the swimming, the climbing, the guns, the arrows. No I fear something else entirely.

An absence that stretches beyond a week into – time

Leaving me waiting

Getting old.

Missing you.

What if?

Stop it, Pen.

Worrying.

He'll just be on a bender.

That's all.

This isn't me.

I don't think you'll recognise me when you get home.
If you get home.
Either way I'll be here.
Waiting.
Oh but this is good:
I cut the plug off that prick Mel's Flymo.

She holds up the plug in triumph.

That'll teach him…
I can mow my own fucking lawn.

Her phone beeps a text and she snatches it up as –

The End.

THE DESERT

DEIANARIA: The Striker
April De Angelis

DIDO: The Choice
Stella Duffy

CANACE: A Good Story
Isley Lynn

HYPERMESTRA: Girl on Fire
Chinonyerem Odimba

SAPPHO: I See You Now
Lorna French

DEIANARIA

The Striker

April De Angelis

Character

DEIANARIA

DEIANARIA	Indra Ové
Director	Adjoa Andoh
Designer	Jessie McKenzie
Lighting Designer	Johanna Town
Composer/Sound Designer	Nicola Chang

DEIANARIA.

It's a bit early for retsina
I don't usually touch a corkscrew till after breakfast
But today's a special day
Will you join me?
Stuffed olive?
These grow on the fragrant slopes of Mykonos. The love island.
Chilli oil gives them a bit of bite.
I've got something I want to share with you.
I'm happy for you to take notes
Or record it on your phone might be best.
What does the world know about Hercules Neville, my
husband? His massive dong and his famous left foot.
Both world-class scorers.
But my beef is this – why wasn't he satisfied with the Ballon
d'Or 101 Man-of-the-matches
And me waiting at home in our circular bed with Lindt
chocolate
Smeared on my nipples?
I mean I'm on the Keto diet I can't eat it.
How could you ask more of a wife?
Faithful?
I watched every match, heart in mouth
Gnawing my nails down to the quick
And they were acrylic.
Would he be wounded?
Would he pull off the Classic Cruyff turn? The Maradona
Scissor
Or the Beckham Bend?
Once when he executed a goal that laughed in the face of
physics I screamed so loud I set off the neighbour's car alarm
And shattered a priceless Lalique standing peacock
Omens.

You were always away, on tour, lapping up hot-stone massages
and more in five-star hotels
While I languished home alone
With the eight-button jacuzzi, the crystal flutes and a set of
gold-plated love eggs.
On return you were more like a guest than a husband.
Whispers of gossip got back to me
Poisoning my atmosphere like second-hand smoke
In my despair I almost gave up Hot Yoga
Why not let myself go?
But I'm a fighter which in case you didn't know you are going
to find out. Okay you went through your teammates' WAGS like
a starving dog
Overdosing on Pedigree Chum.
When you could have had Wagyu steak followed by tiramisu at
home
I could stomach that.
They were passing shags in the night.
Discarded like the crumpled condoms you see lying outside the
24/7 Tesco Metro after a night on the lash.
Forgotten spurts of passion I could live with.
That's on the job description; footballer's wife.
I curse the day you were signed to *Strictly*
I watched her pout at you in the Paso Doble
Tease you in the Tango
Press against you in a wanton Waltz
Your eyes turning to liquid pools of love
Those proud footballing feet, that once kicked out fiercely in
battle
Now transmogrified to tame beasts gently pattering round her
dainty form.

The judges, fools, looked on, smiled and bewitched scored you
tens
The world fell in love with you all over again
As you fell for her.
Headlines in the *Daily Mail*.
Hercules wins the greatest task of all.
Photos I pored over

weeping and knocking back tequila
You two twined together like serpents
A mass of sequins, muscles, manoeuvres.
Knives. In. My. Side.
I've seen you snapped out shopping,
Paddling behind her like a poodle,
Weighted with her bags, like a bloody toothless Jeeves.
You don't smother yourself in Lynx any more she's got you all
Jo Malone
You wear linen
And eat sushi.
Is this the same man that had Ronaldo quaking in his boots,
Rooney saying his prayers
And Messi messing up?
For shame.
She's unmanned you, Hercules Neville.
Everything you won by your mighty deeds
Has now been given up to her.
Your mistress now inherits your great fame.
She was on *Loose Women*, Thursday.
Maybe you want me to drop dead so she can become your wife?
Pine away, find a deadly lump, fatally crash my car on Charlie
Brown's roundabout.
They still tell you, don't they, to get married,
The ivory fishtail dress or the A-line with beads
The bridesmaids standing about like roofless pillars
The salmonella poisoning from the prawn and lemon
vol-au-vents
They never say take a look at the statistics
One in three end in divorce
Many deserted by the faithless fucks that led them to the altar in
the first place.
But I won't be a statistic.
You shamed me.
Me the daughter of Phyllis and Bill Heatherington.
The mother of your child, Darren.
You left me with no choice
But poison. For you and her.
The end of your beautiful dream of playing for LA Galaxy

I was fifteen when you first fucked me.

You said I drove you mad with desire.

You tore off my school uniform.

I can still see it lying there on the carpet thinking aren't we supposed to be in geography?

I know that's the kind of stuff newspapers like to hear. That's why I'm confessing.

What's the point of a god unless he can be dragged into the mud? The greater his goals achieved, the more dizzyingly delicious his fall.

That's the poison I deliver. What a wicked woman.

This is the madness of my love

To watch you being torn apart by scandal. As if I'd pierced you with a blade of steel. Farewell, my lord.

It will be hard for our son to know his dad was a paed.

He'll get that a lot when he goes down the pub.

It'll hang round his neck, like the Olympic gold once hung round yours. But that is the sacrifice I make.

You left me with no choice.

Did you?

They say I'll get to keep the house.

The End.

DIDO

The Choice

Stella Duffy

Character

DIDO

DIDO   Rosalind Eleazar

Director   Cat Robey
Designer   Louie Whitemore
Lighting Designer   Johanna Town
Composer/Sound Designer   Max Pappenheim

DIDO.

Directed by others, I had barely known what I wanted.
I was married to my uncle at fourteen.
Acerbas was Priest of Melqart, the Phoenician god, a good
enough man for a valued bride.
And yes, you might say it was common then, usual then, normal
then.
All very wise,
But no one asked me if it was what I wanted.
It was not what I wanted.
I didn't know what I wanted, I was fourteen, what was to know?
He was an older man, old man, what was to want?
What was it to want?
From virgin to bride, from maid to wife, I was a girl made to
wife.
I wived.

Then my father died, King of Tyre, he willed that my brother
was to share the kingdom with me.
I would share dominion over Tyre, jewel of Lebanon.
Fresh water, the finest port, warm seas and warmer skies, mine
was a home of primeval mermaids, goddesses of fertility.
They all came to praise us, adore us, invade us.
Egyptian, Phoenician and Greek, vying for our trade, dying for
our love.

I was raised to rule alongside my brother Pygmalion.
Our father died and Pygmalion tried to mould me to the shape
he willed;
acquiescent, agreeable, willing.
I would not.
My brother shared nothing but his greed.
He spilled my husband's blood, killed uncle and brother-in-law
in one go.

I left with a ragtag of others and a full fleet of ships
running away
running from
running to
refuge.

Africa was my refuge, Tunis my new land.
He called me Queen of Afric. I am.

At home, I was Elissa.
Here I am Dido –
the wanderer.

Preparing to wander now.

I arrived with nothing but my wits and hope.
I arrived and the land rose up to greet me, opened her arms in
welcome, a rich earth that understood me when I did not know
myself, when I was bereft, broken, grieving a murdered
husband, a traitorous brother and my life ripped away.

I stood on this good earth and made it mine.
In making it, I made me.

I bartered for the land, traded in wit.
Iarbas offered me a parcel not wide enough to breathe, I asked
for more,
he bargained a stretch of land the size of an ox hide.
I agreed.
I can be agreeable.
I killed the ox, stripped the hide, cured it, stretched it, ripped it.
Then I cut the hide into long, fine strips and when they were
laid end to end, I curved them lightly around a corner of coast
outlining what might be as if it were nothing more than a curve
of my gentle arm.
I measured my yet-built city with mathematics, not magic.
I solved the first isoperimetric problem, Dido's Theorem – look
it up, it's real.

I'm real.

And so the land was given to me, ordained mine.
Iarbas had no choice, he was a man of his word, he is a man of
his word.

Word is, he wants me.
And I, a foreign princess, a fatherless, brotherless, widow,
refugee
I dug out these foundations, carved these pillars
and Carthage – *Carthage* – came through me.

I founded a city, this city, a name you know even now.
I built Carthage where nothing was before.
I was twenty-five.

And it was good here, fine here, I loved it here.
Yes, I missed my home and my father and half Tyre that should
have been mine, but I remade myself, remade a Queendom.
And look at it all, Carthage is everything.

Of course, everything made me attractive.
So very attractive.
Men want women and land and gold.
And so, they came.
A thousand suitors, clamouring, stammering, offering, groping.
The port and roads clogged with willing men, wanting men,
wanting me.
I had had a husband, loved a father, hated a brother.
I was tired of men, happy as Dido, only Dido.
I revelled in my building, growing, in the statehood I had
founded.
I had a sister, a friend,
I was not looking for a lover.

They offered, I refused.
Iarbas pleaded, I confused.
Too much abuse.
I was not ready.
The life of a nun appealed
a nun with freedom to build a city, run an empire, live as a
queen.
I became skilled at no.

And then the storm, and then the ships, Aeneas aground.
Here, on my ground.
My Aeneas, six years groundless, stateless, homeless, lost.
Found.

And I'm floundering with love, gasping for air,
Tyrian mermaid in African desert, grasping there
Where
Here
He
Is.

Yes.
Yes he is.

In my arms in my heart in my head in my core in my belly in
my sex
He is all of me, all in me, and I have never
could – never
had – never
I was married to my uncle
I turned down a thousand men
What could I know of this?
This wanting
This desire
Him.

I understand now.
Paris and Helen, I understand.
He is home
wanderer no longer.
I understand.

Son of Venus, he captured my soul
entered my blood
took my body
gained my trust.

I gave him food for his men, ships for his sail, gold for his quest
I gave him Carthage
I gave him me.
He gave me back.
It was good.

It was good.

He stayed for a year, a twelve-month.
Seasons elided and we were in season, he was my season

my taste, my reason.
He was meat and drink, all flavour, where I, parched, had tasted
only water.
Was?
Is.
Is still.

In his arms, I blossomed.
Rose of Lebanon.
Became full and flesh and woman to his half-god, half-man, all
Aeneas.
I, who had survived so much, strived so much,
thrived
opened
flowed
flow.

This is flow, still.
I make choices now, still.

It was not enough time, could never be enough time
I did not know we were on borrowed time, gods' time.
They did.

Meddling, muddling gods.
They cannot bear to see us happy.
Our joy reminds them they are not mortal, there is no end to
their sibling rivalries,
their marital discords – the two-in-one they so often mismanage.
There is no true death to add piquancy to their love,
No then to mean that now is the one moment that matters.
When time means nothing, nothing has meaning.
And so they bicker and avenge, masquerade and descend
to be with us.
But they are not us
and no amount of wearing the animal skin, fish skin, bear skin,
swan skin
can allay their longing.
They yearn to know, as we do,
the exquisite agony of love in time passing
love that sears beneath the skin, burns from inside out

love that counts because death will come –
death always comes.

Pitiful, jealous gods, for whom time has no tide.

And so, he is leaving.
Leaving Tunis, leaving Africa, leaving me.
Mercury came, words were exchanged, Jupiter's message
passed on;
Italy calls, Rome awaits.
And off he goes.

Italy, Rome.
He is leaving Carthage for a swamp.
A city built for one unmade.
A continent of gold for an empire undreamed.
It takes some gall to imagine Africa the lesser compared to a
town sired by wolves.
A willful blindness to turn his back on all this
for that.

From here I can see the ships I gave him, the sails I furnished,
the oars I provided.
They all take him
away.

I could wish him storm-tossed, lost, but he has been lost for
years.
I could wish him run aground, drowned –
But why?
It would not assuage my tears.
I could hold him close, cover his mouth with mine, my breast,
and push the air from his chest
But dead Aeneas would not soothe living Dido.
And so
I have built a pyre of his love.
Gathered together his tokens and mine
The gifts we gave each other, the bounty we shared
The harvest of our love.
And here, at the highest point, the couch where he wooed me,
doomed me to his love.

And he, doomed to mine.
I gave Dido and he gave Aeneas.

When my story is told, I pray they tell of the choice;
the choice to love
the choice to want
the choice to stay
the choice to go
the choice to die

I am not driven mad by love, insane with rejection
I am strong and true
I founded a city
There was nothing here
I made this
I will unmake this
I will unmake me.

Do you see, Venus? Juno? Jupiter?
I can stop pain, break bonds, loose myself.
I can let go.
I'm letting go.

Put this on my grave:
Dido did not fall for a man
She fell by her own hand.
And in falling, she beat the gods.
Let them live forever
I claim my moment
Now.

His sword
Our bed
The pyre the fire of this love.

It is all good
This death is warm and calls me on.

See? There his ships sail aboard.
See? Here I take his own sword.
Sweet Aeneas, you kissed the sword and promised me your wife.
Sweet Aeneas, I kiss this sword and choose to take my life.

My life
My love
My city
My choice.

I did this.
I built this.
I
Do
This

The End.

CANACE

A Good Story

Isley Lynn

Character

CANACE

Note

Words in square brackets are included to clarify the meaning of
the line, but are not said aloud.

CANACE   Eleanor Tomlinson

Directors   Tom Littler and Cat Robey
Designer   Emily Stuart
Lighting Designer   Johanna Town
Composer/Sound Designer   Max Pappenheim

We cannot see or hear who CANACE *speaks to. She starts off calm and smiling.*

No I get it, it is. It's a good story.

Absolutely. I want to tell it.

Yes.

Um I don't know when it started no, um, let me think. Because it wasn't a bolt of lightning or... And we, obviously we didn't, *meet*. But it was pretty clear what was happening. So I brought it up. And he said he loved me. More than loved me. And when he said that... Yeah. I was... Really happy. We were both happy.

(*Smiling.*) I did, yeah. Yeah I've always been quite straightforward. I call spade a spade. I call sexual tension sexual tension. So we had that chat. And we didn't kiss. We decided not to. But then we had another chat and then we did, we, did kiss. (*Laughing.*) And we've both got these noses so we had to negotiate. And another chat, and another chat, but we held off a really long time.

Yeah. We wanted to take this seriously. Look after each other. Make sure that at every stage, every single stage, one of us could tap out. But um. We didn't.

Well we wanted to be careful. Obviously, had to be. And it felt, because normally, because you know who my dad is right? Yeah so I was never going to be able to date or anything anyway. Everything was going to be arranged, to some degree, arranged. So it didn't feel like a big loss, not being able to be a normal couple. I guess I was always, somewhere in the back of my mind, ready? Prepared? For a secret relationship.

No, it didn't, that didn't excite me.

I can, very clearly. He was so nervous. At first. The first time. So was I. He does this thing when he's nervous, it's very cute –

you wouldn't probably wouldn't find it as cute as I do, but you know you're not in love with him, so. Um. I get that other people don't see what I see, obviously I do. I get that. Anyway he was being very, so slow, and we only had until lunch to – it was morning. And I'd bathed. Pretty thoroughly, you know, so I was like 'Come on let's not waste this.' Which, I thought I'd fucked it but he just laughed. I knew he'd laugh. We know each other so well. We just get each other. And uh, yeah, we, well, he, touched my neck. I can remember exactly. Where he touched my neck. And I touched his mouth. And we kissed. The whole while I was thinking 'Remember this. Remember this.' Tried to keep everything in my head so I could replay it because I thought this would never happen again. That he would regret it or I would regret it or we would feel different afterwards. We'd feel, what everyone… Not like, no, we hadn't, obviously hadn't asked anyone, told anyone, at all. At all. No. And we felt, not just good, but better, even better, for having finally done that.

Hmm?

(*Laughing*.) Ah no we grew up together, no it wasn't one of those. Surprise! We weren't separated. No I knew.

Yes both, both parents.

Biological, yep.

No it – no it didn't. No it felt more – I thought to myself 'This is what having an affair must be like.' Which obviously I've never had an affair. Never been married. Couldn't exactly marry each other.

No one loves it. No. No one's super happy about it. I don't know what else to say about that I mean I think it's pretty obvious what they think.

I I, no I do understand why it's weird. For other people. I do get that. I'm not an idiot.

Well I think smoking is disgusting but some people love it so. (*Shrugs*.)

No. You're thinking of twins.

I'm sorry?

The sex? (*Unsure*.) You're asking me if the sex...? Uh...

No go on. I'm fine. No what do you want to know?

(*Strong*.) Yeah. No really good. Actually.

(*Curt*.) Okay.

Average.

Always.

Yes always.

Six sisters and seven brothers, including him.

No! I don't have a thing for for siblings, okay. Do you? Because that's... No. It's not a fetish, that's really important, no, this was, this was two individuals falling for each other.

Well it was all consensual.

No I don't think we were.

No actually I think I'm extremely clearheaded, I think I always have been.

Look, I don't know why you think you're going to give me some great you know insight here. We didn't do any of this lightly, without care, without thought I don't know why the assumption is I'm confused. Or stupid. Or manipulated. Or taken advantage of.

...

Yes, and I'm, and this... Okay. This is what I want to say on that. And I feel so, um, deeply. About what he did. Which came as a complete... A shock. A shock to me. Because before, before it was known, before everyone knew, he was happy. I know he was. Which makes what he did so difficult to understand, his... death, his... And I don't want – this is why I agreed to this because I want to – as far as I'm... it wasn't us, that he, that... it was everyone else. It was everyone knowing. And not shame, not us, not what we were but what everyone... what they made us into. Which we weren't. And I wanted to say that.

I just miss him.

Thank you.

You know what, I don't know if I would. Because when I think back – I mean unless I had somehow the knowledge I have now…? Is that the question?

Oh. Oh. No. I get what you're… but no. No I personally I wouldn't, I wouldn't change / anything about… (*She is cut off.*)

Because I loved him. I loved him for him / for who he was… (*She is interrupted.*)

No not because he was my brother but…

Because why should we!

Because we weren't hurting anyone!

…

… … Um… Yes, yes there was. Who told you that?

I don't want to, talk about that. Why are you – what are you getting at?

No, it didn't. But that's not some… some… Why are you bringing that up? You can't put that on us. We're not the reason…

Of course I'm sad – fuck you!

No, no, fuck you! You want my reaction, you want this to be a fucking discussion conversation you want my fucking response to your – to you saying, bringing up my – my response is fuck you!

I can use whatever language I want I'm a fucking adult. I might be the only one acting like it.

Yes, no, exactly, I understand that, I get that but tried very hard not to have that happen. The lengths I went to. I knew. Talk about 'consequences' the consequences for that would be… We… Which is why we tried not to have one. We tried not to get pregnant. When I was pregnant I tried to get rid of it. And when I had the baby I tried to give it away. Give it a life without us as parents. I wanted it to have a normal life. We didn't want *us* to affect *it*. Give it it's own life, free from... which is all we wanted, all I'm asking for. For us to be just us. And this is the thing I think because it always just felt so fucking unfair. To be honest. Because I do get it. I get why people shouldn't fuck their brothers, trust me. I know it doesn't seem like it. But yeah, that's pretty good advice actually on the whole. I'm not out here advocating – fuck no, no I get why there are laws around it, I get why it can be really bad. Really bad. I'm telling you I get all that, I understand all that. But I am also telling you that it was not that. For us. It just wasn't. I know you look at me and you see a a, abomination a disgrace or shameful, tragedy, which is why I wanted to do this, thought that doing this... That's not what I am. Show you that's not – that's not what this story has to be, automatically. There are exceptions. There are good reasons that our story is a rare one, fine. But there are also good reasons why our story happened. I'm telling you, the reasons, they were good, it was good. It's a good story. A good story. It should just be our story, ours. I want to tell *our* story. It could have been so good.

But why can't it be?

Look the fact is if we could have told anyone asked anyone for help reached out to someone our baby would have lived. So whose fault is that. Who's responsible for those fucking consequences. She wasn't a consequence she was a life!

…

I really think, believe that – I *know* that if everything went to plan, everything would be fine. I *tried* to...

…

It's my one regret. I mean that. My only one. (*Beat.*) We did name her. (*Before they can ask.*) I'm not telling you.

I shouldn't have done this. You were never going to [understand]... You can't.

What?

Oh.

You thought I was here to apologise.

…

You still do.

…

(*Defiant*.) Sorry.

The End.

HYPERMESTRA

Girl on Fire

Chinonyerem Odimba

Character

HYPERMESTRA

HYPERMESTRA	Nicholle Cherrie
Director	Adjoa Andoh
Designer	Jessie McKenzie
Lighting Designer	Johanna Town
Sound Designer	Nicola Chang
Composer	Nicholle Cherrie

The sound of a deep and low jazz bass seeps in – the lament is sung in a jazz/soul-style throughout.

Throughout, HYPERMESTRA *moves and morphs between herself and the chantress – sometimes not knowing which one is speaking.*

The chantress' song appears in italics and right-aligned.

I get to write only one letter to you,
Can you believe it?
So much to say, so little papyrus!
I will have to leave to chance what you read between these words.

> *Lamentations I shall sing.*
> *Incantations to you I bring.*
> *My word shall reach Water, Earth, Sky and Sun,*
> *And beat against your disobedient heart.*

They've employed a chantress…
And as I write, she sits outside the door evoking the gods of peace…
Do such powers exist?
Lynceus, is peace what you seek?

> *Lament for her stubborn soul,*
> *Boldness in SHE took hold.*
> *And her punishment a dirty unworthy hole,*
> *Not fit for beasts less for veritable gold.*

I want to laugh but I daren't as each twitch is reported back to my father.
And all is greeted with the knowing lunacy of men,
Earnest and unnecessary each one of them.
But know that inside I am laughing at their bafflement.

She laughs.

Do not be alarmed by my exuberant energy.
Do not berate me for the contradiction of it.
I know that it is a condition of your nature to do so…
But I urge you to resist…

Beat.

Yes in the face of it, it seems my fate is doomed.
And tomorrow faced with the court of Argives,
My laughter and all joy may be extinguished.
How exciting it is not knowing if I will live or die…

> *Lament for her such beauty corrupted,*
> *Skin flourishing whilst horrors unfold within,*
> *Lament before you become insulted.*
> *Mercy before judgement: let truth's light in.*

And it is that seductive unknowing…
That pleasurable uncertainty,
That place in between that begs me to write to you.
Otherwise I may have decided to turn to the wall of silence…

Such is the curse.

Let me talk to you, Lynceus.
The man who's band I carry heavy around my neck.
Whose branding by name I carry hidden at my chest.
Let me tell you of the girl/creature you have wed.

> *What pours from such a young heart that would betray a father?*
> *What drives a woman to such dereliction and disobedience?*
> *To which god or goddess does SHE worship in such actions?*
> *What makes a life so carefully formed rebel?*

So hear this…
Hear this pen scratching against such darkness…
And then you may decide if this daughter is what you want,
Or the blindness of more lies…

Beat.

The story starts as I reached my tenth year…
Awakening from a kind and peaceful sleep,
And eager to spend another day with my sisters,

Mischievous, we were known for our adventures in gardens of
Aegyptus.

And as it was I find myself, till sleep induced, searching for
morning excite.
Anything that feeds my imagination is welcome.
The song of birds, or the fresh smell of cypress, delights.
Nothing dulls my enthusiasm for such simple things or so I
thought...

I cross the courtyard, pass the fountain and into the arch of olive
trees.
From a low stone wall; I hear what sounds like a fallen lamb.
My heart endears quickly to that sound.
I peek over the edge of the wall sure of animal life...

But what I see is neither soft or...
It is the cry of a young servant girl.
Whose arms splayed asunder moans in a language unknown.
On top of her a man.

She murmurs over and over in her own words.
It is a desperate plea that much I know.
A plea unheard by the creature, who as human as her, but less so,
Grunts over her cries, braying with some awful force.

> *Horror. It is. Horror.*
> *There is ugliness to the scene that I have no words for.*
> *Something brutal I cannot begin to understand yet.*
> *However... I understand something here, and know...*

Long beat.

HYPERMESTRA *kneels – hands raised above her head in
some kind of silent prayer.*

Lynceus, if you are still reading, take courage in my courage.

Beat.

I am a now little beyond my twelfth year...
And assigned to care for a visiting relative wounded at battle.
Being the eldest such is my burden and duty.
To care. To care for. To care quietly...

Such is the curse.

He does not leave his klíni due to his injuries and nightmares,
Yet is fit to drink wine daily from vessels large enough for an
army,
And strong enough to grab at budding fresh ~~titties~~.
Somehow aroused by my protestations.

I am barely familiar with these changes in my own body,
Yet he is already too knowing of their potential... too knowing!
His hands and his attempts grow more insistent,
Until I am forced to feign a sickness to avoid them.

And I am back on my knees at the altar,
Murmuring to any that holds sway and power in the heavens,
Pleading for that unknown girl, for my breasts.
Offering milk, honey and myrrh to distract from the sacrifice
that I may become.

Such is the curse.

But do not despair, Lynceus... not yet...

For the following three turns around the sun, my sisters are my
only companions.
Fifteen and now refusing to leave the sanctity of our home.
Those stories have been told, and my fear infects us all.
Chastity and reclusion is not a choice, but a strategy.

But as you know, soldier, facing the battle can only be avoided
for so long.
And bundled as we are by our father,
Onto the wooden ships made for our escape, on turbulent seas
to Argos,
We are exposed to open skies and curious cruelty.

Imagine it if you can...
Fifty sister-bodies, curled up around each other.
Afraid of the growls of angry waves,
Fifty heavy Danaid hearts unsure of how hungry the sea is.

And suddenly there is forty-nine...
I know because I count each and every one studiously,

Whilst I countenance the thirst in the eyes of ship hands.
Forty-nine....

Terror and tears engulf me.
This is my nature now.
I search the deck blinded by salty water not sure if from mine
eye or the sea...
Calling the names of gods and sister in equal rhythm.

And there, in the radiance of the moon,
My sister taking kisses across her hands, face and neck...
I watch unsure when to pounce... if to...
The kisses seem sweet even to my eyes.

Innocence seeming back in favour,
I uncurl my tendons and start my breath.
Barely for a second... barely fully at ease...
When the suitor's hand reaches for her...

~~Cunt!~~
What a ~~cunt!~~
In a flash I am at my sister's side, her hand in mine,
And the other arm disposing the perpetrator into the dark sea.

The next day I am counting more carefully...
One less man onboard...
And we sail on...
We sail on to here.

> *Lament for the one they hold inside.*
> *Gods that be see her heart still alive.*
> *This young woman, child, bride...*
> *Your song is my song, my song yours to testify.*

And, Lynceus, this is where you come in.

The contract of marriage was not my choosing.
But a daughter's word is a daughter's word.
My only say was in how...
You see I chose the weapon.

Such is the curse.

A vision I had conjured up in this sweet head so many times
before.
A revenge for each of us to slay our drunken and helpless
grooms.
Fifty brides for fifty violent sons.
A dagger seemed fitting somehow...

Yet you that night as you lay so near to me,
A wall of pillows between us,
On your insistence,
On your promise... you...

My vision moves away from your perfect smooth neck,
And the crimson blood that will spurt from it gladly.
My hand, shaking and hesitant, around the grip of that blade.
I hold tighter to all those memories of being burnt but...

A cacophony of contradictions rages inside me.
What was I to do?
Hypermestra...
What are you doing?

> *It was hard to say then,*
> *But how formed it is now.*
> *How much the words spill from SHE loud...*
> *How she spits them out with resolve and power.*

I spared you for no other reason than my own.
You were like a rare bird captured mid-flight.
Like a hope manifest and possibly... possibly...
Is it possible that you could live to speak that decency to other
men?

If this promise can be made real...
Then your life was worth saving...
And my sacrifice...
(Yes it seems that is what I have become after all...)

Let it be decided by men no matter what.
For these years of folding myself into myself,
Is a curse I have broken well.
And remember what she asked –

What pours from such a young heart that would betray a
father?
What drives a woman to such dereliction and disobedience?
To which god or goddess do I worship in such actions?
What makes a life so carefully formed rebel?

I am in my sixteenth year,
Barely in such womanhood but fully in my mind.
I have already lived a life of full of dread...
The lamb that knows the cries from the slaughterhouse...

A girl who knows that women's throats get slit.
Tender bodies get splayed.
The light in women's eyes can be turned to dust.
And that WE get burnt by the endless cruelty of it all.

This new Hypermestra cannot be bound by invisible fears no
more.
She wakes up.
Is woke.
If she shall die let me die too... in divinity... in all justice, in this
world...

A woman's life should never be cursed by the dishonour of
men.
This I willingly lay myself down for.
Oh Hypermestra...
Oh goddesses of war.

Lynceus, know that the wedding band that sits on your person,
Belongs to a girl that spoke her truth.
A girl that faced those flames.
A girl finally on fire for her life!

Beat.

PS Sorry about your brothers.

The End.

SAPPHO

I See You Now

Lorna French

Character

SAPPHO, *a Black British woman in her fifties or early sixties.*
Sappho is a well-known national and international singer

Setting

Sappho's bedroom in her flat in Moseley, Birmingham, UK.

SAPPHO   Martina Laird

Director   Tom Littler
Designer   Emily Stuart
Lighting Designer   Johanna Town
Composer/Sound Designer   Max Pappenheim

Summer 2020. SAPPHO *sits at a dressing table. There is a
mirror in front of her. This mirror is imaginary and faces out to
the audience (so that when* SAPPHO *looks in the mirror she
actually looks out to the audience). There is a bottle of English
Rose perfume by Yardley, assorted make-up, make-up-remover
wipes, a pair of scissors, a heart-shaped vase, matches and
some photographs on the table.*

SAPPHO *puts a letter into an envelope and starts to seal it
shut. She pauses, uncertain if this is a good idea. Finally
making a decision,* SAPPHO *takes the letter out of the envelope
and spreads the pages before her. She smoothes down the pages
and screws up all of her courage. She begins reading her letter
out loud to check it over one last time.* SAPPHO *begins by
holding and reading the pages of the letter, but after the
'Sapphic verse' section, she puts down the letter and continues
to recite without it.*

I write to you but I'm not sure; will you recognise these inky
marks on pink pages? Pages scented with your favourite
perfume. Each sheet sealed with a blood-red kiss at the bottom
just for you. I worry you won't recognise the loops of my
handwriting. That even after all our time together I must sign
my name to this to jog your memory.

I know what you're thinking. If you recognise the writing my
trembling hands have attempted, you're wondering why I've not
sent my words to you in my usual song lyrics backed by strings.

*The following is spoken with the rhythmic structure of Sapphic
verse, with stress placed on the syllables in italics and those
syllables in roman being unstressed.*

I am *wi*-dely *known* for those *mu*-sic *pre*-tty *ly-rics*,
But my *woe* is *not* suited to *mel*-o-*dic* notes *from strings*,
Gui-tars, *vio*-lins *with* ly-ric *num*-bers *end here.*
E-le-gy *suits* prose.

My tears smudge the ink as I write, betraying the throbbing flames in my heart, that burn like a bitter harvest that will eventually turn to ash.

Our unsuccessful love makes my uneasy mind unsatisfied. Having lived in Trinidad, my mother's country, I came to you young, eager, open, and with a longing to make a life in the country of my father. Back home in Trinidad they called your country the mother country, but I never did. To me it was the place of my father; where he voyaged to serve and work and make a life. The place he had learned to love. As soon as I landed; sixteen, still childish but eager, I learned to love it too. It was home to me. For years I exiled myself from my mother's island shores and clung to you with all of my heart. My years in Trinidad didn't leave my memory but it was with you I'd staked my life, my love, my future, my all.

You enchanted me with the myth of your exceptionalism. You were the epitome of all things; lifestyle, education, manners, everything. You were the ideal for me. When I first came you called me to you, encouraged my flirtation with you. Then you were happy with my education, my skills you swore you couldn't live without. As years went on and my singing became uppermost for me and I gained world renown, you looked at me with such tenderness when I sung in your name. I no longer sung for Trinidad; I sung for you, representing you where ever I went.

You loved me then, even though I wasn't blessed with ideal beauty. My lyrical notes sung in husky tones, that have been lauded the world over, were enough for you then. Even though I am not blonde, my eyes are not blue and I am not model thin, the accolades I won for you were enough. Weren't you pleased with Naomi Campbell and Beverley Knight, though their skin is closer to chocolate than to the fairest, blondest blue-eyed lady? Doves of different colours often unite. We were once entwined in love and need for each other. Or so I thought. You couldn't get enough of every word I sang. You often stopped my words to reward me, as long as I was singing to glorify and exalt you. But now you've turned from me, turned hostile to me and those who don't share the Whiteness your eyes are enamoured with.

What can I do with my melanated skin and African hair that will turn you from your new love back to me? How can I change myself to be who you desire again? I cannot! Oh why do I lack perfection in your eyes?

Beat.

But, Britain, I now find that you're faithless. You once again honour the far-right winds that spread the catching flames years ago to Brixton and Handsworth and Toxteth. Fuelling those who would equate Britishness with Whiteness.

Beat.

For those who would make your home in this deceitful isle, as I have, beware. This country of my father has a tongue that lies. It pours sweet nothings in your ears about streets paved with gold and green and pleasant lands. But it's a forked tongue; whispering of welcome and advancement when you're in far-off places and Britain's in need. Don't be deceived by the faithless vows that were made to me. I was once where you are now. Learn from my story. If you don't, the elegant empty words that woo you from your home to these shores could put you in my place in years to come.

My hair is no longer inky black curls; it instead hangs permed straight and blonde. My nose is contoured to accentuate its thinness and my skin bleached to a lighter shade that pleases you better. My perfume is your favourite; English Rose.

SAPPHO *studies her reflection in the mirror.*

But I look and look and look. Now that I'm deserted by the country I love, who's all of this for? This chasing European beauty standards I'll never meet, just so I won't lose your love. Years of disguising features in me that you couldn't bear leaves me a stranger to my reflection. I may usually be a genius with words and melody but I have no words to name what I've made myself to please you.

Beat.

You abandoned me with no fanfare or noise, just a single letter. Branded me illegal immigrant and that was it. There was no kindness in it. Ties I'd formed over decades ripped from me and my life crumbled to dust. Go home you said. Scar tissue has formed on my heart from that blow. Go home you said. I swayed unsteady like a storm-stricken voyager clinging to a flimsy vessel in a sudden storm. Go home you said. You broke the contract I manage through tears. There's a social contract: you were in need and I came to your aid. Supported you, built you up. The only thing I asked is that you be mindful of me. That one thing I asked of you. You wouldn't do it.

SAPPHO *looks at her reflection. After a moment she uses make-up-remover wipes to take off her fully made-up face. SAPPHO rubs desperately to get it off, but then is more controlled and begins to slowly but methodically remove every drop of make-up.*

I realised too late that Britain cannot love anyone that is not a direct reflection of Whiteness. Not wholeheartedly, not sincerely, not without critique, complaint and cruelty. Not right now but, even after such ill-treatment, I hope one day you can.

SAPPHO *rips up photographs and throws the pieces into a heart-shaped vase.*

Mute, beyond any reach of Cupid, discarded by fate and love, I ripped up pictures of myself in beautiful sequin gowns singing all over the world to honour what I thought was my country. I ripped up pictures of my sister in her nurse's uniform tending Britain's sick for years and years. I ripped up the one picture I have of my father standing proudly in his RAF uniform, fighting for King and Empire in 1942.

SAPPHO *uses matches to set the pictures on fire.*

I ripped at my clothes and thought only of what I could've done to be such an object of hatred to you.

SAPPHO *removes her blonde wig, revealing her natural cane-rowed hair underneath.*

Your cruelty, your go home, your hostile environment have finally convinced me that I should no longer ask for your love. Tears soak the paper now as I write. I do not ask you for love now and cannot give you mine.

The Fates have plunged me off a cliff into the rushing waters below. But I come up again coughing and spluttering.

Beat.

I'm different now, baptised anew by the waters that could've been my demise. So, Britain, though I'm without your love now – (*Beat.*) I can live.

Beat.

The waters I've been plunged in wash off the performing versions of me created just for you. Clinging to the riverbank now, as the waters rush by me, I look at my reflection in the rippling river water. It's slightly blurred still, blemished with tiny traces of the lightened skin that pleased you. But those will darken again in time. I keep looking until the river surface is smooth as a mirror and my features stop shifting. Cupid's arrow must hit me then because I catch sight of myself as I really am. I'm not as White or blonde or thin as you demand, but I'm enough all the same. No, I'm not just enough; I'm beautiful. I'm ideal.

SAPPHO *stares at her reflection for a moment.*

Lights down as SAPPHO *continues to examine her features in the mirror.*

The End.

THE LABYRINTH

ARIADNE: String
Bryony Lavery

PHAEDRA: Pity the Monster
Timberlake Wertenbaker

PHYLLIS: I'm Still Burning
Samantha Ellis

HYPSIPYLE: Knew I Should Have
Natalie Haynes

MEDEA: The Gift
Juliet Gilkes Romero

ARIADNE

String

Bryony Lavery

Character

ARIADNE

ARIADNE   Patsy Ferran

Director   Tom Littler
Designer   Louie Whitemore
Lighting Designer   Johanna Town
Composer/Sound Designer   Max Pappenheim

ARIADNE *is discovered with a ball of string.*
She is whipping the end of a sharpened piece of wood...
She is not wonderfully good with her hands...
She's more at home with books than real life...
She's an incredibly entitled snob about anything not royal and
Minoan...
She barely has her head above the terrible soup of anger, grief
and regret she is swimming in.
She looks up and sees us.

Aaaah!

She watches us intently.

Are you friends?

We don't speak.

Are you foes?

We don't speak.

Are you gods?

Of course, we don't answer. We just watch her.

You're here to observe me.

She is most used to being silently observed.

I understand.
I will try to inform.

She realises she may need to explain what she is doing...

I don't *know* this country
'Naxos', apparently....?
I've *zero data* on its people and animalia
So...

She continues to whip the stick's end...

A stable boy at our palace taught me this when I was nine... it's called 'whipping'...

She whips...

He was *whipped* in quite the other sense of the word for his teaching me *this* meaning of whipping...

This amuses her a bit.

This gives me *grip*...
If a... (*Whatever terrifically new, unnamed and scary person or animal attacks her... lots of possibilities to an imaginative young woman.*) *whatever* animal
Comes at me...
I can... (*Some impressive dagger-lunging and stabbing... Actor's choice of sounds for...*)
Unngh! (*Heart lunge.*)
Fsstt! (*Throat-cutting.*)
Mnnninkkk!!! (*Disembowelling.*)
One should *always* carry a ball of string.

The ball of string takes her brain to the dreadful event... so... eventually.

...because one never knows when someone you've trusted *utterly*...
And love more deeply than *the wine-dark sea...* is going to slither off like a *jackal*, leaving one 'post-coital-sleeping' while he boards his ship and fucking fucks off marooning you in utterly strange and unknown alien friendless territory!!!
This is the very ball of string I gave Theseus to navigate in and out of the Labyrinth!
It was by our bed when I woke.
Neatly rewound.
Look.

She shows us. He's done a very neat job.

He was very good with his hands.

She nearly bursts into tears.

And his mouth!
'Darling... you are my bright my clever rescuer!
Let us make sweet love then sleep and at dawn we'll board my
ship and go tell my father how you saved my life!
(*Miming.*) Here's your string back!'

(*Bursting into tears.*) Sorry.

Princesses should be *impassive* in public.
People with both royal *and taurine* blood shouldn't...
Blub like *cheap whores...*

Is this safe?

You should know... *Naxons...*
I'm daughter to Minos of Crete.
My mother is Pasiphae.
I'm *Ariadne*
Which derives from '*ari*' – 'most'
'*Adnos*' – 'holy'
The gods *should* protect me!

But no sign visible as yet.

However...

(*Imperious.*) I *have* betrayed both my family and my country so
it is as yet *unclear* quite *what* the gods have in store for me here
in deeply wretched and so-far-*featureless* 'Naxos'.

*Gods can come at you from any direction, but their favourite is
the air...*

My family and the gods have always *enjoyed,* if that is the right
word, a highly competitive and rocky relationship.
So, I anticipate spitefulness and quixocity!

Beat.

I *know* it should be 'quixoticness' but I like to make up my own
words sometimes!
I apologise for this *internal tumult.*
I am *trying* to breast the stormy whirlpool of deep dread,
incandescent fury and sea-green *shame* to reach the shores of.
Calm.

Self-forgiveness.

Indifference.

I'd like to be dead.

Back to the task.

I have to think about *this* to not think about the veritable
Hellespont inside me.
It's called 'avoidance'
I've also, this is my first visit *away from home* you see... got a
touch of 'separation anxiety'...

Her teeth chatter so...

You lash the end of a piece of wood to keep it from fraying.

She applies herself to whipping until...

It seems not to stop one's temper from fraying.

I wish I were home.

No, not home!
I cannot, of course, go home
If you breathe in the air surrounding me, you will smell all my
boats burning...

But...
Time is a Great Healer apparently.
That's what my tutor Daedalus says...
But... how long does the great healing take?
How long's a piece of string?
How long to get over someone who's clearly been stringing you
along?
You see how I extemporised with string imagery just now?
I'm *famously* bookish
My brother called me 'Ink Blot'
And Theseus 'Big Balls'
So I said if that was what he called Theseus I would call *him*
'Bull Balls'
My brother.

Don't think about it.

Here's some things you can do with string...
Parcel things up so you can't see the truth of them any more.
Follow it into a dark place

Don't think about it...

Lash the end of a piece of wood to keep it from fraying!
You've already said that
None of this is my fault.
If *Daedalus* hadn't started me thinking about 'string', I'd *never* have come up with all this...
Daedalus who made his son Icarus some wings so he could fly?
Feathers glued with wax?
Icarus who flew too near the sun?

A mime of a boy plummeting into the sea.

Why by all the gods did I allow myself to be led by a man who couldn't see how *that* would end????

A helpful history lesson.

Daedalus designed the labyrinth...
And, it now turns out, *the inside of my brain*!!!...
His 'string theory'...
'I have this theoretical framework, Ariadne, in which all the many-dimensional particles of everything in our universe are replaced by one-dimensional objects called "strings".'
'That's *Princess* Ariadne,' I said
'In everyday life we inhabit a space of three dimensions... like a vast storeroom with height and width and depth...'
He was grieving for his boy so I said, just to deflect him...
'We could consider time as an additional fourth dimension.'
And he said
'You are a very clever little girl, Ariadne.'
And I said
'I know. And it is "Your Royal Highness".'
And then we were forever making 'strings' to explain the fundamental interactions of the universe
And life was sweet and educational in a lovely *non-painful* way!
We even did experiments with '*time*'

We tried to travel *back*
We tried to see into the future

There may be a knot in the string.

Aaaah!
Here's some things you can't do with string.
Tie someone up so they can't leave you.
He *promised* to take me with him.
We had a *deal*.
My father says 'If you make a deal, *keep to it*, especially with
men and even more especially with *gods*, otherwise, you'll end
up like your mother and I, with a *bull* for an heir!'
My father often exaggerates for dramatic effect.
My brother is only *half*-bull.
Theseus said
'The string idea is *brilliant*, Ariadne.
But.
I need a knife as well.'
I said
'For what?'
He said
'Protection.
Just in the unlikely event I run into anybody or anything.'
Theseus is a *classic hero*.
He *has* to run into things.
That's his appointed *fate*.
I pretended not to but I *knew* that.
And I know my brother.
Knew my brother.
I knew how it must end.
One of them had to die.

A shameful admission.

I wanted it to be my brother.
The Minotaur.
Who was half-man. Half-bull.
Utterly disgustingly hopelessly ugly.
But… How could you not love a brother who was this silly
snorting stamping goofy hoofy parody…

Sorry… (*Another clever bit of wordplay…*) lost my thread for a
bit there…

Here's what you cannot do with string.
Moor a ship so it can't leave without you.
Tie someone forever in your bed.
Make a new brother.
You need boy bits and a lot of beef and spittle and
…and he needs to be breathing.

She's realising her brother is really truly dead.

You cannot unravel string across the sea
And find your way back to the centre of your labyrinthine
family…
You cannot go back in time…
Daedalus and I practically *proved* that…
But
Before I left
We were exploring the possibility that
One can exist in differing realities…
I'm here with you now making a weapon for protection
But
I'm also
At home
In the great hall
Explaining myself to my father and his lords of counsel
And
I'm also
At home
But
In the women's palace
Curled round my beautiful mother
Begging her forgiveness
And
I'm also
Standing with Theseus on his ship
As it sails into the harbour of Athens
The black sails billowing in the breeze
The seven strong boys and the seven beautiful girls

Un-sacrificed
Intact
Alive...
And I'm saying to him
'You must change those black sails for white
So your father knows I have returned you safe to him.'

The makeshift dagger is whipped.

There.
Come, Eagle!
Come, Sea Lion!
Leviathan?

There are no eagles, sea lions or leviathans as far as the eye can see...

I need to practise on *something*.

She stabs it experimentally into something at hand.
The dagger breaks.
She bursts into tears of anger and frustration.

It's hopeless!
I am *hopeless*!
This wasn't for protection from wild animals.

She throws it away as hard as she can.

It was for Theseus.
I was going to *practise* on eagles and sea lions and leviathans
So my *technique* would be *faultless* when I plunged it deep into
Theseus....
There's veins in the human body...
They're like strings with blood in them.
I was going to take them all out of Theseus...
When *he* was post-coital-sleeping...
Make them into a ball.
Hand them to his sister
Say 'Here. Go find *your* brother.'

When I went to the epicentre to... to look at *my* brother....
His stomach was torn open

By Theseus
By the dagger I gave Theseus.
What was remarkable Was. His innards. His guts. Inside.
Looked like a labyrinth...
my brother had the labyrinth inside him as well as outside.
Was his inside always like that?
Or, did it become that because we made him live there?

She looks at her hands.

My hand is bleeding
The veins are like strings just under the surface.
Look.
Strings with blood in them.
What can I do?

She thinks.

My mother slept, unknowingly, tricked...

A new discovery...

Possibly tricked...

This is a little bit funny...

Hah...
with the king of the gods
I have some of the gods' ichor flowing through me...

She grows in stature somehow.

Theseus forgot me.

She uses her arms to receive power...

I wish him
Another lapse of memory

She becomes taut as a wire...
Incredibly focused as...

Theseus
I enter your mind
So
For a moment

You remember me
You are sad
You miss my warm teachable body
My quick mind
And...
....

She reaches across the sea to Athens...

Theseus...
Forget to tell your men to change the black sails for white
And
So your father sees the black sails and thinks
'My son is dead'
And his heart breaks in two
And he dies
For this is the curse of Ariadne
Ari
Most
Adnos
Holy
And her strongest weapon is not this pathetic stick
It is her wonderful, her far-reaching mind.

The End.

PHAEDRA

Pity the Monster

Timberlake Wertenbaker

Character

PHAEDRA

PHAEDRA	Doña Croll
Director	Adjoa Andoh
Designer	Jessie McKenzie
Lighting Designer	Johanna Town
Composer/Sound Designer	Nicola Chang

PHAEDRA.

This is my name: Phaedra.
You cannot say it. Or will not.
Phaedra.

This is my body: a woman
Who has children
A little younger than you.
You cannot look at it. Or will not.
A woman not young, not a girl, and so to you what?
A monster?
Fearsome.
You might turn to stone if you look.

This is my history:
Married to your father the Athenian.
You know that much.
From Crete: next stop Africa.
Lands you do not wish to know.
That could tangle you in their darkness.

This is my heritage:
A mingling beyond the human. You would say beneath.
You will have heard myths, you call them rumours.
A god turns himself into a bull
To attract a girl.
Monstrous attraction: strength and beauty and savagery.
And gentleness too, when an animal loves a human.
My grandmother.
And then my mother
Perhaps bored with the human
Gives birth to the Minotaur, my half-brother, yes.
Half-human, don't forget.
Until your father, with full human help and full human wile

Kills the monster.
Without pity.

We are not the animals you can kill in the hunt and eat, but we
are not the humans you can accept. We are the monsters.
The ones who cannot join that exclusive, that oh-so-desirable
club: the human. Blackballed, branded and barred. Your
membership is unquestioned, you were born into it, you dwell
happily there, mingle with those who are like you. The normal.
Obedient to the norm. Man is the measure of all things, you're
fond of saying. And what are the other 'all things'? Stars,
planets, animals, plants, insects. Or gods. 'Of the things that are
and of the things that are not,' you say. And of course of the
things that should not be and therefore, to you, cannot be. You
don't look or you quickly turn away. We are not there.
The undefined and undefinable.
We who don't make the human grade.
The monsters.

Your own membership is unquestioned. Hippolytus. Son of
Theseus. Son of Aegeus. Untarnished Athenians all. Normal.
Obedient to the norm.
For you no intermingling, no cousinship or fellowship with the
non-perfectly human, the messy and badly marked borders of
being. We who spill out of your narrow confines, break your
rules, the decorum of control and what you call self-control,
that is, human control.

And now you ask

How dare this monster approach you.
Request your attention.
How dare this monster look at you, the pure human, with
longing?
How dare this woman feel desire?
Even request a return of desire.
Monstrous.

You don't look.
Or if you glance you quickly turn away –
What can a monster offer you, you the perfect human, male and
beautiful? And young. With what words can I persuade you to

hear my monstrous thoughts? To open your human mind, and i
your human heart, take in the monster. See her. Hear the
monster, pity the monster and then even love the monster.

We roam that other world. You have borders against us, barriers,
definitions. You lock us out, you think you're safe.

But who is locked in? We make do with the wilder shores, ragged
peaks, sunburnt lands, untilled, unorganised, unmeasured, but,
how to say it, not beautiful no, that is very human, let us say
fascinating, enchanting: you've never been here.

It's not a place you might hunt animals, kill them for sport or
food. It is where you and the animals might look at each other.
No longer obey the differences, the norms of hunt and flee but
rather stop and look. And listen. Differently shaped in body and
mind, perhaps not bound by reason, by the human rationale, but
that is not all that needs to be heard.

Think of how we are: always eager to trust you, believe you,
always admiring of you, susceptible to your beauty. Your
perfect humanness.

But now, turn around, stop demanding praise from us. Stop
assuming we deserve our humiliation. Or more often, our death.
Turn and see what we have to offer you. What you define as
monstrous. Look again.

Think of your horizons: how narrow they are. Always aspiring
to be perfect and more perfect, tighter, more reined in. So little
curiosity about what other worlds are on offer, what other
shapes – what other experiences? Man to man, ordered, always
defined, bound, ruled, closed. The supple and the subtle
changing of forms escapes you.

You seek perfection and try to breed perfection. All in good
order. But consider for a moment disorder. What might it be?
What would happen if you let go?

You obey rules. The human rules. Handed down by generations.
Rules to restrain, keep you in order.
What if you disobeyed? All those boundaries, lines, rules,
prescriptions, blinkers and prohibitions shaken off –

ɪ? Content in your realm. Animals to hunt and
ʌnded down and feelings to be controlled.

ᴛhe delight of experience, of the new, of the
the strange, of the monstrous.

You ʏ.   ⁾ be like your father. That is? He seduced my young
and trusting sister and then abandoned her; killed a first wife,
your mother, well, that's what they say. He rules a hollow and
well-ordered kingdom. Your father hunts women, you hunt
animals, all equally trusting and in awe of you. But turn, turn
around:

Here is the forbidden: the wife of your father. Not young,
indeed to you old, not perfectly formed, spilling out, in shape
and feelings, a woman, the unknown, uncontrolled. Think of the
adventure. You could leave yourself, your rules and your fears
and find courage. Yes, monstrous courage. Not overcoming the
fear of human death, striding forward into war or the hunt.
Rather allowing yourself to melt. And as the human oozes out,
you, for the first time you will really have no fear.

I'm not asking for what you call love – only an acceptance of
desire, and what is desire but curiosity, the question: what is
here? What is this? How can I know it?

That is wealth. Not conquering more humans but a world
unknown, unseen, unsuspected even, our world as it is,
unbridled, multi-shaped, full of passion, richly coloured, a
treasure trove of the overlooked, the mystery of the unseen.

Pity the monsters.
Pity is the ability to look at what you do not want to see. And
when you can look, the norms change. And when the norms
change, the rigidity of judgement and distaste melts.

Pity is the emotion you have never known, forbidden in your
world, too dangerous, too messy. Yes, pity takes you into
another world, pity is a merging of limbs and heart, of thoughts
– it shapes itself into a wave, drawing the shoreline back to
itself and then bursting. That is pity.

Find in yourself this pity, fall deep into another world. And you will see it was always there, right there, under and around you, deep, broad, different, multi-hued. That world will receive you and it will transform you –

Come, come close, without restraint. Be curious, turn around and see the monster, listen and approach. I'm here. I will not shed my skin for you but I will clothe you in mine. Come to me: I will save you from the human.

The End.

PHYLLIS

I'm Still Burning

Samantha Ellis

Character

PHYLLIS

PHYLLIS	Nathalie Armin
Director	Cat Robey
Designer	Emily Stuart
Lighting Designer	Johanna Town
Composer/Sound Designer	Max Pappenheim

PHYLLIS *is an eastern queen from a long time ago. She is here now, with trees and flowers and tendrils hennaed on her hands and face.*

I never even wanted to fall in love. That's the truth.

Not *my* truth; *the* truth. There's a difference. This is my story. This is *the* story.

She lights a candle. Music starts.

I was always one of the girls. When it came to paint the bride with henna, we would hold candles and make a circle, dance around her.

Music starts. She starts to belly-dance, slowly, for no one but herself.

We were young and beautiful, with our candles and our long hair. And then I didn't marry, and I didn't marry and I didn't marry, and I was not a girl any more but a woman, but still not married, still holding my candle, dancing round the bride, and smiling because I didn't envy her a bit.

The music fades.

For *years* they tried to marry me off – to save them from the horror of being ruled by a woman. But I wanted to rule my country *and* myself.

And I was good at it. I knew what to do.

A storm blows up. It blows out her candle.

When there's a storm at sea, go to the shore, look for boats, search and rescue. I direct the operations myself. I look good in a high wind. Get the men in! Get them indoors!

Storm sounds cut. We are indoors.

And there you were.

All beaten up, and ruined, and – despite a bit of water damage – *hot*.

And younger than me. You only had power because of who your father was. And right then you had nothing. That was part of the appeal. You weren't strong. You weren't arrogant. You had come from the war and you were bruised and battered, hurting on the inside too.

There were things I needed to forget.

Men I needed to forget.

I looked after you. It made me feel so powerful. Like a witch who could heal. And I did. I healed your wounds, I patched your clothes, I washed the salt from your hair. I gave you wine and bread. I cooked for you: lamb and pomegranates, rice and lentils, almond milk sweetened with dates.

My arms softened and I ached to hold you.

My heart opened.

I wanted you and I took you.

And when you were stronger, you said: let me look after you. And you pulled me to you and the heat of you. The smell of your sweat. The heft of you. Just leaning on you I felt safe. I felt home. And I thought: this was it! This was what the songs were all about! All the stories!

And you said: let's get married! The gods can be our witnesses! I was so impressed! Gods as witnesses! I should have got some actual, human witnesses. Witnesses who could watch you make your promise, and shame you when you broke it.

Music starts up and we see candles moving around PHYLLIS *in the dark. In the centre she dances, a bride.*

The night we slept together, the Furies were shrieking in the dark. Birds who hate the light were singing miserable songs. Snakes were hissing. We lit our bedroom with candles stolen from a grave. I didn't care. This was a love story. I was its heroine. And I wanted you so much.

Did we get married?
You say we didn't.
I say we did.
In my culture, if you sleep together that's promise enough. Even without words.

But there were words! You were full of words.

You swore by the sea – the inconstant sea! Never trust a man who swears by the sea. Especially don't trust a man whose grandfather *is* the sea.

Because then you said you had to go. Urgent business, you said. Your father, you said.
Even then I believed you. Because you made a promise that was so precise! You said you'd come back by the next full moon.
I waited four months.
I never counted days before I met you.
I lied to myself that you would come.
I cursed your father for keeping you away.
I imagined you dead... but in a nice way!
Because you promised to come back. And you were not back.
So you must be dead.
Because this was a love story.
And because we are always slow to believe what's going to hurt us.

I wish I'd just fixed your ships, and not your broken heart.
I wish I'd given you safe harbour in my actual harbour, not in my bed.
I wish I'd died before you came.

What did I do except love unwisely?
Why did you promise undying love? Why did you curse the winds that were taking you away? Why did you crinkle your brow and take me in your arms and hold me tight and tell me to wait?

When you didn't mean any of it. You were never going to sleep in my bed again or swim in my sea. You didn't even want this country *which I gave you*.

Did you think I would just wait?
I did wait.
I waited because I loved you more than anything.
I waited until I was sure you'd forgotten me, forgotten my name.

And there I was. Ghosted! Me, a queen.

* * *

I thought about death. I thought about poison, or a knife, or a noose around the neck you used to kiss. I thought I'd get them to write on my grave: you murdered me. Or better: because of you, I killed myself.

I was burning.

I'm still burning.

It's been millennia and I'm still burning.

I thought the sea would put out the fire of my rage. I thought I would walk into it and keep on walking till I drowned. Till the waves smashed into me and filled me up. I pulled you from the sea, half-dead, and gave you everything. If I came west in a leaky boat, what would you do for me? If I washed up on your shore, bloated by sea water, eyes eaten out by fish... what would you say? You'd make a joke: You shouldn't have followed me like *this*, Phyllis!

* * *

People were angry. They said I'd lied. They said we weren't married because you said we weren't. They said you boasted about having me. I was a liar and a whore, and they didn't want a queen who lied and slept with soldiers.

This isn't just a love story; this is political.

They told me to kill myself. To be a tragic dead queen, mourned and pitied, not a live one, wailing on a beach.

If you kill yourself, they said, you'll control how the story ends!

But why does it have to end? There's still so much I want to do.

There were demonstrations. There were riots.

And the women rose up and said: We believe her.
Is that it? They believe me and that's supposed to be enough?

The women said: Just tell everyone what happened.

Everyone loves a true story.

Tell your story and there will be poems.
There will be hashtags.
There will be a country right behind you.

And I refused.
Because why should I parade my humiliation for anyone?

It was mine.
It happened to me.
And mostly in the dark.
And I was ashamed.
Ashamed of being lied to.
Ashamed of being left.
Ashamed of being alone.

* * *

I should have told my story to everyone I met. I should have
painted it on walls and shouted it from rooftops. I should have
written it down. Before anyone else did. Before any men did.

Ovid.

He called me a heroine but he made me sound *miserable*. And
everyone praised him. For writing the women's point of view.
Giving us a voice. Making our stories heard. Centring our pain.
You do have to ask: why did he write so many women? Why
were all his women abandoned or pining or wounded or raped?
Why did he write so many rapes? I know why he told my story.
He thought he was cleverer than me. He said: 'Phyllis would
have survived if she'd had me as a teacher.'

Her *teacher*?

Chaucer. Chaucer put me in his *Legende of Goode Women*. I've
got no interest in being a good woman. He said 'The only man
Phyllis should trust in love is me.'

Ovid wanted to teach me. Chaucer wanted to fuck me.

At least Apollodorus didn't want me to be a good woman. He wanted me to be a witch who would take a lover and give him a magic box and say: don't look inside until you know you aren't coming back. And on that day, and not before that day, open the box.

Apollodorus said, when you opened the box, what you saw was so *terrifying* that you leapt on your horse and rode to your *death*. Or you ran so fast you impaled yourself on your own sword.

Neither seems likely, to be honest. Your horse was just there? Your sword was just sticking up out of the ground?

The only reason you'd open the box is if you knew you weren't coming back.

I didn't think you were ever coming back.

* * *

I can't explain how I did it. Only that the bark started creeping over my skin because I wanted it to. And, I thought: *yes*.

Make me hard. Kill what was soft in me and make me strong so I can live.

PHYLLIS *changes her stance, planting her feet more solidly. She starts to raise her arms.*

Maybe I was a kind of witch. Maybe I did have a kind of power. My arms became branches, my fingers became twigs and my feet... my feet pressed the ground, pressed down hard and suddenly they were reaching down, down, down into the soil and I was drawing up this... *energy*. This sap, this strength, this power – from women! From all the women in the earth. I was *surging* with it. My veins were singing. *We* were singing. There was tearing, pushing, leaves and flowers and wet green came bursting from my mouth and my roots spread far and wide, and I was planted. I took up so much space. I called the wind and it came rustling through my leaves.

PHYLLIS *shakes out her hair and leaves fall all around her.
She is a tree.*

* * *

The truth is: you *did* come back.

Let it go on the record: I was not abandoned. You came back.

And you knew you'd done wrong because when you saw me,
you burst into tears.

* * *

And when you came, I burst into blossom.

Because this is a love story.

But this is not a love story.

She is realising this right now, and it hits her with some force.

It's never been a love story.

I burst into blossom through sheer joy.

Because you couldn't have me any more.

The End.

HYPSIPYLE

Knew I Should Have

Natalie Haynes

Character

HYPSIPYLE

HYPSIPYLE   Olivia Williams

Director   Tom Littler
Designer   Louie Whitemore
Lighting Designer   Johanna Town
Composer/Sound Designer   Max Pappenheim

HYPSIPYLE *writes a letter.*

Dear Jason,

I hear your ship is safely in Thessaly. Are you rich now? Finally got your hands on that golden fleece? I'm glad you're safe, I genuinely am. It's just – I really think *you* should have written and told me all this? I definitely should have heard it from you. I mean, I'm sure you were racing back here to share my kingdom, weren't you? The kingdom I promised you. But perhaps you didn't have a favouring wind in your sails. Still, though. A letter can be written no matter which way the wind blows, can't it? Or apparently it can't. But I deserved some sort of message.

So why, Jason, did rumour reach me before I heard a word from you? Rumour which says, incidentally, that you – let me just check, because I wrote this down. You should give it a try – that you yoked bulls sacred to the god, Mars, and ploughed a field with them. And then you sowed seeds which produced – and I feel like I'm making this up, but it's what the rumour claimed – a crop of men, who killed each other without you lifting a finger. Oh, and after that? An unsleeping dragon guarded the fleece you nonetheless managed to steal. Oddly, some people seem sceptical of this story. Do you know what I'd like to be able to say to those who don't believe it? 'Jason wrote this in a letter to me himself.'

But why am I obsessing that my husband hasn't written to me? If I'm still yours (and you're still mine), I wouldn't mind. But the rumour is someone left the island with you: a barbarian woman, a poisoner. She's sharing the bed you promised me. Love makes me believe anything, but I hope for both our sakes this isn't true.

Recently, some Thessalian arrived here. He was hardly through the door before I asked, 'How's Jason, how's my man?' His voice stuck in his throat with shame, his eyes fixed on the ground. I ran at him, tearing at my clothes with the nails I used to tear down your back. 'Does he live?' I screamed. 'Because if he's dead, I'm dead.' 'He lives,' the man replied. Someone in love is always full of fear. I forced him to swear it was true.

He's the one who told me about the bulls with their bronze feet (actual bronze? You have to admit it sounds insane), about sowing the teeth of a snake in place of seed, about how armed men suddenly rose up out of the ground, fought one another, lived and died in a single day. He told me about the snake you killed. Again, I asked if you could possibly have survived – fear and hope.

He races through your exploits moment by moment, he's excited. Right up to the moment where he breaks my heart. My god, Jason. Where's the loyalty you promised? That bloody wedding torch, should we use it to light my funeral pyre now? Should we use your vows as kindling?

It's not like we did it in secret. Juno was there, goddess of marriage – remember? Hymen too – god of weddings? We had good guests, Jason. Hymen dressed up specially. But you know what? Neither of them carried the wedding torch, did they? That was left to the Furies. The bloodstained, baleful Furies.

I never cared about your damn ship or your men. And none of them gave a shit about me. Well, why would they? I don't have a golden fucking fleece, do I? So you had no reason to come here: I don't know why you ever did. And I should have seen you off like I was planning to at first. The women of Lemnos know exactly how to treat men like you. Our menfolk know it even better. Knew it, I should say.

But some evil fortune stopped me from giving you what you deserved. Damn it, I should've let my army of women rise up and defend their city, their queen. And instead, I saved your life, kept you safe in my palace, in my stupid, trusting heart.

You were here for two years: two summers, two winters. But then when the third harvest came along, you made your excuses – you had to set sail. You wept as you spoke. 'I'm being ripped

away from you, Hypsipyle! As soon as the Fates allow it, your
man will come back here to you; I will always be your man.
And the baby growing inside you, please god, let it live. And
then we can be parents together too.'

Tears flowed down your false face. You were the last man to
climb aboard the *Argo*, just before she began flying across the
water, wind in her sails. As she cut through the waves between
us, you were gazing back at the land, I was gazing out at the
sea. I found a rocky outpost, waves breaking on all sides, and I
sat there and wept until my face was soaked. I was so desperate
to see you one last time, to find you through my tears, I stared
after your ship. And as I cried, I added prayers, sacrifices that
the gods would keep you safe for me.

Am I free from those prayers, those sacrifices now? Am I?
Because it's Medea who gets to enjoy their results, not me. My
heart hurts, and my love is tainted with anger: they rush through
me together. Do I take offerings to the temple, because Jason is
alive, when he is lost to me for good? Must I keep making
sacrifices, giving thanks for my injuries?

I never felt safe loving you, I was always afraid that your father
would want a Greek for his daughter-in-law. But now it's some
fucking barbarian whore who causes me this pain. I wasn't
expecting the pain to come from that direction, I can't lie. She
doesn't deserve you, she isn't even pretty. She doesn't need to
be: she's used magic to win you. She can stop the moon in its
tracks, hide the sun in darkness. She can bring woods to life,
move great rocks if she chooses. She stalks the dead, her hair in
a state, stealing bones from still-warm funeral pyres. She makes
wax figurines, and stabs her sharp pin into their wretched livers.
It's probably safer not to know any more. Let me just say this:
the love she wanted, she won with her potions. But I didn't need
any herbs or spells. We shared our love because of my beauty,
because of my soul.

How can you touch a woman like that? How can you even be
alone with her? Aren't you afraid to sleep beside her in the quiet
moments of the night? She's got you under her yoke, just like
those bulls. She's tamed you just like she did the snake.

She wants her name written beside your heroic deeds. Her name. She wants her fame to outshine yours. And you know what? It will. Someone could easily say that she was responsible for everything, with her poisons and potions. They'll say that she seized the golden fleece, not you.

And your mother won't like her, by the way. So let her find someone else. You're as changeable as the weather, Jason. Your words have no weight to them, your promises are worthless. You were my husband when you left, and now you're someone else's? What is the attraction? Her famous family? I'm the granddaughter of Bacchus, an actual god. I outshine her in my ancestors as well as every other way. And I would have given you Lemnos, my home, as my dowry: this gorgeous fertile land. In addition to my home, you would also have me.

Oh, and though you haven't asked, I did give birth. No, don't bother congratulating me now. Congratulate us both! Because we have been blessed with twins. If you're wondering who they're like, by the way, it's you. Well, they're not fucking liars. But otherwise, they're exactly like their dad. In fact, I almost sent them to you, so you'd remember we exist. But then I got scared of their vicious stepmother. Who knows what she would do to them?

Didn't she tear her brother limb from limb? Scatter his body parts across the ground? But she's the one who's made you mad (with her poisons, no doubt). She's the one whose bed you preferred to mine. It disgusts me. She betrayed her father, I kept mine alive against all odds. She deserted Colchis, Lemnos holds me still. But perhaps you prefer her wickedness to be the dowry you receive. Who knows with you? I'm not shocked by the crimes of other women, Jason. Say, the women of Lemnos, my women, and what they did. They were mistreated so they rose up. That's different. What's her excuse?

Imagine you'd sailed back here, as you were meant to. Entered my harbour, like we'd planned, except with your new companion alongside you. What would you have said when you saw me, when you saw our children? And – tell me – what do you think would have been a just reward for your treachery?

You would have been quite safe, though. Not because you deserve it, but because I am nice. But I would have covered my face with the blood of your whore. Your face too, which she stole from me with her spells. Ha – I would have been Medea to Medea.

So if Jupiter above is paying heed to my prayers, let him visit my pain on her, and more. So as I am abandoned with two children, let her lose her husband *and* her children. Let her lose everything she stole, and let it happen soon. Let her lose her home, let her flee, no safe haven anywhere. This vicious sister to her wretched brother, vicious daughter to her wretched parents, may she prove just as bitter to her children and her husband. Let her seek refuge in the air when land and sea have rejected her. Let her lose everything, even hope, as she flees, covered in the blood she has spilled. I pray for this.

Now live with it.

The End.

MEDEA

The Gift

Juliet Gilkes Romero

Character

MEDEA

MEDEA	Nadine Marshall
Director	Adjoa Andoh
Designer	Jessie McKenzie
Lighting Designer	Johanna Town
Composer/Sound Designer	Nicola Chang

Darkness. A candle is lit. The flame flares and illuminates
MEDEA. *She solemnly places the candle on a table. She stares*
into the light...

Sister. Amongst our people we say if someone is banished, it
means they have died. But when they return, if they return, we say
they are back from the dead and we rejoice in their rebirth. That's
if they haven't already vanished from the lives of those they love.

MEDEA *drops to her knees.*

I beg you, remember that I lived. Because here they are killing
my name. You will read and hear terrible things spread about
me in the press. Believe nothing. Know that what comes next is
born of my free will, not the wild actions of some weak,
lovelorn, jealous woman. And yes, the bare bones of my exile
are known and cannot be disputed. But the flesh with which
generations of hate-filled men will choose to cover them... well
that is a different matter.

A beat.

I married a mercenary I despised and yet I loved him.

A moment.

Sister. I'm not asking for your pity, the gods know I don't
deserve it but I need you and all I see is your face set like
stone... a death mask and the huge empty eyes of our ancestors,
staring from the gloom behind you.

A moment.

This morning, Jason sent his 'people'... thugs.
This loudmouth barking orders, grabbed me by the arm and
earned himself a good slap. He gripped me by my throat.
'We're not here for you. It's the two bastards we want.'
As if my sons were nothing.

A moment.

That's when my heart… and time itself stopped. And the unholy curse upon me… shattered. I launched blows at this devil and roared, 'I am Medea. Princess of Aea. You do not touch my boys!!'

A beat.

Stunned, he tackled and brought me down, hard. My head hit the floor. My body followed. There was blood and I felt myself losing consciousness.

MEDEA *wipes away a tear.*

Sister. I miss home. Our people. Our gods…

She looks up and into the flame, waiting, hopeful.

Jason got me good. Women here in Corinth are not only trapped they are completely invisible. No right to own property. No right to choose a husband. No rights over their children. Of course Jason thinks I'll put up and shut up while he cavorts with his pubescent, new bride. This… Princess Creusa… The child's hair is the same colour as the golden fleece. My fleece. My dowry. My destiny. My passport to becoming queen. Not only did Jason squander my birthright, he's seized a breastless, half-woman to replace it!

A beat.

People have died for this… this… obscenity! My people! And without me, Jason would never have had the bloody fleece. It was me who slayed the serpent charged with its protection. I who climbed the rocks behind the creature's lair and attacked it from behind, cutting its neck with my poison-tipped hunting knife, while Jason and his idiots pissed themselves with fright. The fleece is mine!

A moment.

Sister. Jason destroyed our family. Justice demands that I destroy his.

A beat.

(*Contrite.*) Yet my stomach clenches with the dread of it. Oh, you think I'm weak? Why won't you speak? Or is silence your revenge? Show yourself!

MEDEA *scans the darkness. She lights a second candle.*

Do you remember my first kill?

A beat.

All you could hear was ominous quiet except for the sound of our footfall as we tracked the doe, and Father insisting, 'Medea, show respect for your prey. Make the end swift. Squeeze the trigger,' he said. 'Breathe.'

A beat.

My twelve-year-old self, fingers shaking, raising the rifle, aiming and somehow taking the shot. The zip of the bullet, tearing into bone and flesh. The doe stumbling into the clearing, collapsing, silent, bleeding, blinking.

A beat.

The doe's young, behind the trees, staring at their mother, confused, afraid, waiting for her to move...

MEDEA *finally breathes...*

I've made arrangements. Me and the boys will travel light and at night. We'll be smuggled aboard a cattle truck as far as the coast.

A beat.

I hear rumours that I, the Barbarian Princess, eat the eyeballs of my enemies. Good. I am happy for them to believe this. I hope they run a fucking mile.

A beat.

I should have run when Jason and his lackeys swaggered onto our shores. Entitled. Unruly... (*Ashamed.*) Exhilarating...

A moment.

The curse itself was cast by a woman. Hera they called her. Some spy attached to Jason. This Hera possessed peculiar

powers of persuasion. It was Hera who spirited me aboard the
Argo, poured far too much wine. It was Hera who seduced me
with her 'holy mission to spread wealth and civilisation'. I was
intoxicated but it could have been the booze. 'Let us join forces,
I'm talking rich bilateral ties,' she said. 'Let us help you reward
your people with the bounty of enlightenment.' Now the witch
was talking hot trash but I began to see Jason, beside me in
magnetic and irresistible new light! The man glowed like gold.

A moment.

The next day, I found myself bound for opportunity, milk and
honey, alongside the stolen fleece which Jason had convinced
me was necessary to make me queen... Several months later, our
arrival in Corinth... the stuff of legend. Immense crowds spew
into the streets. They scale balconies, rooftops, lamp posts just to
gape at the great entourage of the celebrated Argonaut as he
ushers in his prize bride with her swollen, pregnant, black belly.

A beat.

Sister, I was immortal.

A beat.

It didn't feel like a curse, until they came to take my two boys
away. (*Confused.*) Perhaps there was no curse at all? Perhaps
Hera was a phantom conjured by guilt-ridden sleep?

MEDEA *shakes her head.*

I am no traitor. I'm sure of it.

She lights a third candle and stares intently at the flame.

No goddess now but black witch. Evil temptress. Murderess.
Barbarian slut. That's right. I've killed women and children too!
I've killed just about everything that walks or crawls! I strip
naked and take off down the boulevard, streaking, bare-skinned,
like a crazed chicken that keeps going after its head's been cut
off. Bawling obscenities at my cowardly oppressors, 'I'll
destroy you ALL!'

A beat.

What!? It's true.

Laughs.

Actually, it's not true but this story gets in the papers anyway and everyone consumes and gets fat from it like locusts in stretch pants. Truth has long since vanished like cigarette smoke, leaving its ash.

MEDEA *sits back.*

After Jason's thug knocks me out, I regain consciousness. I feel pain but not physical pain, like a crushed ankle or gouged eye... I feel soul pain.

A beat.

A commotion outside announces his arrival. Jason enters defiant, flanked by two bodyguards. 'She is much altered, sir. Wild. Stand back.'

A beat.

Jason hesitates. There's something in his eyes... shame? A residue of love for the mother of his sons? 'It's over,' he starts. 'The hysteria, the terrorist threats... The King wants you gone. I'm taking the boys,' and he snatches them like loot.

A moment.

When you are desperate you forget the dignity you know. You are even forced to forget there is dignity to be forgotten. I drop to my knees. I beg. I beg for one more day. Just one with my children. I prostrate myself before him, weeping bitterly at his feet. Jason stumbles back. He's unable to endure such tears and quickly hands my boys back.

A beat.

I praise his abundant humanity and assure him that the gods will reward him for all eternity. I crawl under the bed and pull free an exquisitely wrapped gift... 'Happy birthday!' I cry.

A beat.

Jason and his 'people' stare at me dumbfounded. One of the
thugs eyes the package. 'What the hell is that?' He demands. 'A
little something for the party... spun from the finest Aean gold
and more precious than the fleece itself.'

A beat.

Jason is flattered. He raises a gracious hand to stay his attack
dogs, 'I've always said that mercy bears far sweeter fruit.
Unfortunately, the King does not see it this way. You must still
leave Corinth. I can give you until tomorrow.' And just like that,
Jason takes the offering and exits, his entourage trotting and
fussing behind him.

A beat.

Barbarian.

A beat.

I gather the boys and we're ready to flee. But I hear the sound
of police sirens, wailing like babies in distress. The kind of
noise that makes you sick.

A beat.

Fate is not done with me. Breaking news. It seems Jason's
return to the palace is brought to a premature conclusion. His
greedy wife, jealous of the birthday present, foolishly snatches
it, unwraps it, flings it open... whereupon the contents, plastic
explosives, explode.

Silence.

This parting gift was not meant for the child bride. I bear the
idiot no malice.

A moment.

My face is set as hard as stone. They will be coming for me
now.
Outside, there are two thugs, murderous, weapons drawn,
running straight back into this building.

MEDEA *looks over at her sons.*

My children are deep in the sweet oblivion of peaceful sleep.
Even as they dream they are angels carrying our forbearers into
the future by golden chariot. They will not take us alive.

MEDEA *reaches for a firearm. She checks it's loaded and looks
out the window.*

If I hold steady, I can get one clean shot. But that leaves the
second.

A beat.

Sister. Speak. I don't know how this will end. But, it's likely to
end badly.

Hearing the gunmen enter, MEDEA *quickly blows out the three
candles and closes her eyes. The room is in darkness.*

I am home in the mountains of Aea. The doe stumbles into the
clearing and collapses. I run over to where it lies bleeding,
blinking. That's when I see the doe's young, huddled behind the
trees, staring at her, confused, afraid, waiting for her to move.
They depend on her for so much love, guidance and protection.
Now that is all gone.
'Medea,' says Father. 'Finish it. Allow death to come to the
dying. We are not barbarians.'

MEDEA *breathes. She cocks her weapon. Then the sound of
two shots ring out.*

The End.

A Nick Hern Book

15 Heroines first published in Great Britain in 2020 as a paperback original by Nick Hern Books Limited, The Glasshouse, 49a Goldhawk Road, London W12 8QP, in association with Jermyn Street Theatre

Introduction copyright © 2020 Natalie Haynes; Individual plays copyright © 2020 April De Angelis, Stella Duffy, Samantha Ellis, Lorna French, Juliet Gilkes Romero, Natalie Haynes, Charlotte Jones, Hannah Khalil, Bryony Lavery, Isley Lynn, Sabrina Mahfouz, Chinonyerem Odimba, Lettie Precious, Timberlake Wertenbaker, Abi Zakarian

The authors have asserted their moral rights

Cover image by Ciaran Walsh

Designed and typeset by Nick Hern Books, London
Printed in the UK by Mimeo Ltd, Huntingdon, Cambridgeshire PE29 6XX

A CIP catalogue record for this book is available from the British Library

ISBN 978 1 84842 986 4

www.nickhernbooks.co.uk

facebook.com/nickhernbooks

twitter.com/nickhernbooks